CLOTHIER OF THE ASSABET

Edward Carver Damon

Clothier of the Assabet

THE MILL AND TOWN OF

Edward Carver Damon

RENEE GARRELICK

Second Edition
© Copyright 1988 by Renee Garrelick
ISBN 0-9618872-0-6
Library of Congress Catalog Card Number
87-090968
Book Design by David Ford

Contents

Facing the Millennium

During the past decade since *Clothier of the Assabet: The Mill and Town of Edward Carver Damon* was first published, the intended goal of introducing a new dimension of history in the context of Concord's commercial past, has been achieved with gratification. The integrated lives of a mill owner with Concord's leading nineteenth century literary and intellectual figures, remains a continued source of fascination and a distinctive aspect of the story.

The successful renovation of the mill and listing on the National Register of Historic Places visually presents a continuum between history and commerce. So many times the remarks were made, "if this information didn't exist our image of Concord would be so different." Historical preservation and business interests, too often perceived as separate and clashing, have notably complemented one another. Without business support, *Clothier of the Assabet* could not have been published and the knowledge shared.

The continued interest in *Clothier of the Assabet* has been further stimulated by the current opening of the Concord Museum's major exhibit, "Why Concord?," which includes extensive use of materials from the book. Damon was a founder of the museum, and today two presidents of Concord's leading businesses, Richard Spaulding of Spaulding & Co and Robert Quinn of Nuclear Metals, Inc., follow his service as board members. With the decision to keep the book in print, I turned to both companies for assistance and they generously responded as they had for the first edition. But this time I wished to transfer my long admiring association to describe their own contribution to Concord's commercial life and history.

As renewed life came to the abandoned buildings of Damon Mill, Richard Walbridge Spaulding watched with admiring interest and experienced understanding of the effort required. As a history enthusiast and devoted preservationist able to see things as they could be, Spaulding has applied his vision to revitalize many a community's landscape. From the restoration of old schools, barns and farmhouses, to tired and decaying Main Street structures, to an effective blend of contemporary function with a building's period architecture and surrounding terrain, the quality of Spaulding's work has made a difference.

Meticulous research precedes restoration, and Spaulding's interest has benefitted Concord Center's Milldam to preserve and adapt its buildings for current use. Along the multi-use rough and tumble Virginia Road, he has created a Vermont visage for Concord Farms, a modern office park that shares the ambiance of the company's restored historic eighteenth century farmhouse, and a renovated barn for corporate headquarters.

"We are on the threshold of what has been called 'The New Metals Age,' and the challenge to develop new materials stretches far beyond such fields as nuclear energy and space technology to the whole new industrial civilization we are creating."

> *Dr. Julius Stratton, President of the Massachusetts Institute of Technology, at the Dedication of Nuclear Metals in Concord 24 October 1958.*

Few companies have been so welcomed to Concord because few companies were so sought after. In the years following World War II, Concord was looking to develop a more balanced economy and attract industry, while the school committee was looking to broaden the tax base and build a new high school. The efforts of the Development and Industrial Commission established to conduct a search were considered well rewarded in finding the right match for Concord. "Nuclear Metals is the kind of company we have been seeking for this land," formerly the site of the powder mills in Damon's time.

Founded as the metallurgical laboratory of M.I.T. in 1942, NMI was acquired in 1954 by Arthur D. Little Co., who named their subsidiary to reflect the era's optimism in a nuclear future. The move from Cambridge to Concord and the dedication of the new facility in October 1958, was filled with excitement and abundant media coverage. The media seemed fond of comparing NMI, as a pioneering company of the space age with Concord as the birthplace of a new nation. John F. Kennedy, then a Senator from Massachusetts was the keynote speaker, and projected the promise and vitality of new beginnings that was his inspiring vision two years later with The New Frontier. Poised at the new technological frontier, "prophecies of New England's decline, its quiet sleep, its pallid future," would be reversed, said Kennedy.

Privately owned since 1972, the excitement of intellectual discovery and material development for aerospace, medical, defense, and industrial needs continues to define NMI as it probes the frontier of the twenty-first century.

Renee Garrelick,
Concord, Massachusetts
1997

Remnants

On 8 October 1943 Alice Damon at age seventy-five married for the first time and left her Concord home for California. Her house, which still stands at the corner of Main Street and Old Stow Road, was one of the homes built by Col. Roger Brown, a Minuteman in the Battle of the Nineteenth of April 1775 who owned extensive property in the western part of Concord. She left the scattered remains of family history—principally the diaries of her father Edward that encompassed a twenty-year period beginning in 1862. Crowded into the pocket diaries are pencilled references to national and local happenings, work and family life, and occasional miscellaneous memoranda. The diaries were part of Edward Damon's very being; he relied on them for his own past records and noted the times they almost slipped from his pocket.

The diaries are not self-serving; the concise phrases do not embellish an event nor extol its author. The constancy of Damon's recordings makes it highly probable that there were diaries other than those which remain. Those that have survived are fragile fragments of history, which when supplemented by letters, memoirs, and town records of the period become the transports to a past era when Damon's textile mill dominated the commercial life of nineteenth-century Concord. The materials that have remained in the private collection of the Damon family are partial and casual, stimulating many questions of what may have been even as they contribute to that knowledge.

The traditional image of historical Concord is not one of mill life and a thriving commercial past. Yet such mill life did exist in harmony with Concord's pastoral farming community. Its expanding commerce a source of community pride, the mill was a major employer and energetic stimulant to the economy, and its owner Edward Carver Damon, a prominent town leader.

What emerges then is the unexpected blend of landscapes and lifestyles—the mill owner faithfully attending the Lyceum lectures of his friend Ralph Waldo Emerson; the advocate of education serving on the school committee with school superintendent Bronson Alcott, while sharing teas and talks of temperance with the strong-minded Louisa. Nature is found at the site of industry in the descriptive journal entries of the flora and fauna observed by Henry David Thoreau in preparing survey maps of the mill for Damon.

The diaries and personal letters of Damon record a time in which a bitter Civil War put an end to slavery in this nation, the Industrial Revolution took hold, and a mature factory system developed. It was an era when immigrants arrived in large numbers; there was widespread use of child labor and a twelve-to-fourteen-hour workday. But it was also a time of reform when the loftier visions and writings of the transcendentalists gave the town its literary legacy.

By the end of the century when the Damon Mill closed, New England had lost its dominance in clothing manufacture as the industry moved to the South. The last use of the mill for textile manufacturing ended in 1923 when the Strathmore Worsted Mills closed after two decades of occupancy. The mill subsequently became an apple and cold storage facility, the buildings deteriorated and by the mid 1970s were abandoned.

By that time the memory of Damon's mill had faded and its very existence was threatened as local stirrings began to call for its demolition. But even with the site near ruins there was a grand strength to the structure that drew interest. A link with the Damon past was Edward Damon's great-grandson Richard, who lived close to the mill in the home built for his grandparents Ralph and Mary. The seeds of rebirth were sown following a backyard conversation between Richard Damon and neighbor William Sullivan who had an interest in industrial development. Forming the Mill Square Partnership, they purchased the site following a public auction on 1 September 1977 and began the slow process towards multi-commercial use for small owner-occupied businesses.

The decay that threatened to seal the story of its past forever was now reversed. In 1980 the Damon Mill was listed on the National Register of Historic Places. Beyond the physical refurbishment of post, beams, and bricks, the time had come to probe for the life and era of Damon's mill when the entire site worked in unity for the conversion of its bales of raw cotton and fleece to the cloth of function and fashion.

I was first shown the diaries of Edward Carver Damon in August 1985 at the time of publication of *Concord in the Days of Strawberries and Streetcars*, a portrayal of earlier twentieth-century life through the memories of longtime residents, which I wrote for the town's 350th birthday. Once I began reading the diaries I soon recognized that here too was an added dimension for the record, emanating from the commercial rather than what has traditionally been perceived as historic Concord. I began the research buoyed with the excitement of using sources that had not been published before. The flavor of Edward Damon's era is presented through a topical narrative that relates the life of the mill to the surrounding town.

I am indebted to the spirit of partnership—business, town, and civic— whose financial assistance brought this book to completion. To each sponsor and donor my heartfelt gratitude.

With a camaraderie formed from our previous book effort, Jane Benes, David Ford, David Little, Nancy McKinney, Alice Moulton, and Peter Orlando, once again brought their respective areas of expertise in guiding this manuscript through production. Curators Marcia Moss and Joyce Woodman of the Concord Free Public Library provided invaluable assistance in the midst of building renovations. My appreciation to Tuska Benes, Mary Callaghan, John Collins, and Rosita Corey for their special contributory efforts.

The presence of a book at all owes so much to Ann Damon's patient support in collecting and making available family owned materials for my use. I entered her home an interested researcher and left as a friend. My thanks to the two Henry Damon families, both great-grandsons of Edward Damon, for the use of family diaries, and to Farnham Smith and Shirley and Stephen Smith for materials relating to Henry Francis Smith. And as ever my loving gratitude to my family, who once again had to postpone the puppy and bear my distractions.

Renee Garrelick,
Concord, Massachusetts
1988

CLOTHIER OF THE ASSABET

"D' ye think, said Mr. Dooley, "tis th' mill that makes th' wather run?"

(Mr. Dooley, "Casual Observations," by Finley Peter Dunne 1867–1936)

True Grit and a Quiet Spirit

Traditionally the "lords of the loom" have not inspired affection. Work in the mills, synonymous with the grim exploits of the Industrial Revolution, stirs strong empathy instead in literature and song for the operatives. Distanced from the workplace, the image of the mill owner is singularly equated with the quest for profits.

For Edward Carver Damon the historic evidence dispels such portrayal. He was an active presence at the mill and participated fully in the civic and intellectual life of the community. He emerges as an individual with strong personal ethics, a deep spirituality, and responsibility for the less fortunate. Family concerns are never far from his accounts of the mill. While Damon faced with stoic calm the destruction of the mill by fire, he showed emotion openly at the loss of those close to him, as with the death of his brother Willie during the Civil War and his young daughter Bessie at the time of the centennial celebration.

Born 19 July 1836, Edward Damon played an active role in the community from early adulthood when such leadership rested with a small core of the populace. It was an era when democracy had a narrower definition, symbolized by the poll tax as a requirement for voting, a measure discriminatory against the economically disadvantaged. Annual town reports often show the same names regularly appearing in town office and on committees.

Damon's involvement and the respect in which he was held become worthy of note because of the geographical distance in which he lived from the center of town. Anne Damon was an educated partner for her husband, and with her active role in school committee matters, husband and wife often made the horse-and-buggy trip to the center of town together. Through service as

A.º Sorgato   Venezia.

Anne Damon. Active in the cultural life of the community,
she was elected to the school committee before the women of the
town could vote for that office. (Courtesy of the Damon family)

TRUE GRIT

Henry Francis Smith, cousin and mill partner of Edward Damon.
Their strong town leadership roles closely paralleled one another.
Circa 1912. [Courtesy of Farnham Smith]

school committee member, selectman, and road and water commissioner, Damon grappled with the key issues of his day. "His voice and wise counsel were always heard in our Town Meetings," recalled his cousin and partner for twelve years, Henry Francis Smith. "His townsmen without doubt, would at any time have chosen him to represent them in the state legislature, if he had given the slightest intimation of his willingness to do so."

In 1866 at the age of thirty, Edward Damon was elected a member of Concord's prestigious Social Circle, founded in 1782, whose twenty-five male members were among the most influential in town affairs. The memoirs written about deceased members have proven to be a valuable source of town history. Henry Francis Smith wrote the biographical memoir about Edward Damon, whose influence in town affairs he closely paralleled. His election to membership, according to Smith, was "strong testimony to the regard in which he was held, especially considering how far he lived from the other members of the Circle." Damon regularly attended the Tuesday evening meetings and noted in his diaries which member was the host and how many were present. In 1900, conscious of his deteriorating health, Damon chose to host the first meeting of the season on October 2. "He felt better for the effort, knowing that it would be the last time," reflected Smith. Damon died three months later.

For thirty years Damon was a director of the Middlesex Institution for Savings and the Concord National Bank of which he became president. Community responsibility for the indigent centered on the public almshouse, and in 1871 Damon was part of the committee to supervise the design and building of a new one for Concord. If it was William Munroe's desire to build Ralph Waldo Emerson a proper town library to work in, the venture required many planning meetings prior to its opening on 1 October 1873 with Damon's diaries showing him in regular attendance. "Been to dedication of the library," he wrote at its opening. "Received photographs of the library from William Munroe." Damon served on the first library committee and contributed generously to the growth of its collection.

The long workday did not preclude other interests for Damon and expectations for those he employed. The hall above his counting room held a library and was a place for religious services and civic and social gatherings that included his efforts at organizing a village improvement association.

Concord's well-known writers and artists were active participants in the community and the Damons shared their company. For transcendentalists Bronson Alcott, William Ellery Channing, Ralph Waldo Emerson, and Henry David Thoreau, nature was a projection of the spiritual, and each individual carried a divine spark. Individualism, a love of nature and the movement to social reform which challenged all existing institutions to become more humanitarian were its accompaniments. The very optimism and promise of the American experiment endowed each individual with a spiritual power where personal integrity and civic responsibility could flourish.

Many of the transcendentalists were well-educated Yankees from the Boston area with training in the Unitarian ministry. Education had a social purpose; scholars did not retreat from the world but were actively involved, their exchange of ideas stimulated through conversation. Alcott's School of Philosophy became a summer adult forum that drew many of its participants from outside of the community. The transcendentalists had faith in the ability of mankind, appropriate to the optimistic expansiveness of the America they inhabited. They represented a philosophy of idealism, where insight into nature did not mean turning their backs on the developing technology, but a refusal to allow that technology to control them—the mind and spirit of the individual were too important to succumb. Within this context industrial advancement, the free enterprise system, community activism, and humanitarian reform were in accord.

Anne and Edward Damon frequently attended the Lyceum lectures at the Town Hall, with Ralph Waldo Emerson a clear favorite of theirs. Damon proudly recorded that his 1875 lecture "On Eloquence" attracted "a full house." "Mr. Emerson gave one of the best lectures this evening," he wrote on 18 February 1874, "On Greatness." Damon was sufficiently moved by what he had heard that two days later he called on Emerson to request passages from the lecture that evaluated what made men great. Emerson obliged and the written pages that bear his signature remain today in the Damon family. His own lack of pretense found expression in Emerson's words: "You shall not tell me that your commercial house, your partners or yourself are of importance: you shall not tell me that you have learned to know men: you shall make me feel that. Your saying so unsays it. You shall not enumerate your brilliant acquaintances, nor tell me by their titles what books you have read. I am to infer that you keep good company by your better information and manners: and to infer your reading from the wealth and accuracy of your conversation."

A sensible person will soon see the folly and wickedness of thinking to please. Sensible men are very rare. A sensible man does not brag, — avoids introducing the names of his creditable companions; drops out of his narrative every complimentary allusion to himself; omits himself as habitually as another man obtrudes himself in his discourse, and is content with putting his fact or theme simply on its own ground, and letting Nature bear the expense of the conversation.

You shall not tell me that your commercial house, your partners, or yourself are of importance: you shall not tell me that you have learned to know men: you shall make me feel that. Your saying so unsays it. You shall not enumerate your brilliant acquaintances, nor tell me by their titles what books you have read. I am to infer that you keep good company by your better

A friend and admirer of Ralph Waldo Emerson, Edward Damon regularly attended his community lectures. He was sufficiently moved by Emerson's description of the qualities of a great man, to request its passages. 1874. [Courtesy of the Damon family]

In July 1880 Damon wrote that "Ralph has been to town at reception at Dan French's studio . . . Miss Emerson spent the afternoon here and Ralph has taken her home this evening . . . Anne went to the philosophy class (at Bronson Alcott's School of Philosophy) and heard Mr. Channing." That year the Damons attended Emerson's one hundredth lecture in town, titled "Historical Notes of Life and Literature in Massachusetts." They were among the guests invited to an evening of tea, mysticism, and conversation at the home of the Emersons where they joined Bronson Alcott, William Ellery Channing, and Prof. William Torrey Harris, the first Commissioner of Education. Damon information and manners: And to infer your reading, from the wealth and accuracy of your conversation.

———

Whilst degrees of intellect interest only classes of men who pursue the same studies, as for instance, chemists or astronomers, or mathematicians, or linguists, and have no attraction for the crowd, there are always men who have a more catholic genius, are really great as men, and inspire universal enthusiasm, a great style of hero, who draws equally all classes, all the extremes of society; till we say the very dogs believe in him. We have had such examples in this country, in Mr. Webster, and I should say in the Seamen's Preacher, Father Taylor. Abraham Lincoln is perhaps the most remarkable instance of this class that we have seen; - a man who was at home and welcome with the humblest, and with a spirit and practical view in the times of terror that commanded the admiration of the wisest. His heart was as great as the world, but there was no room in it to hold the memory of a wrong.

R. Waldo Emerson

described the evening in his entry of 1 August 1880. "Mr. Alcott spoke, then Dr. Channing, then Mr. Alcott again and Professor Harris—all were excellent and I quite entered into their spirit." The letter of invitation for that evening from Ellen Emerson to the Damons still remains. Ellen Emerson and Anne Damon shared an active involvement in school affairs, each serving on the school committee before members of their sex could vote at Town Meeting.

Social occasions were shared with Louisa Alcott and her sisters. "Attended party that included the Misses Alcott. Had a fine collation," Damon wrote on 12 August 1869. The following evening the Damons held a dance at their home, "called on the Misses Alcott and they came down," the next day Damon visited with Louisa Alcott and she in turn "took tea" with the Damons. At this time, Damon's account of his reading included a newly published book by

Ralph Waldo Emerson with grandson Charles Lowell and son Edward Waldo.
The child died in infancy. Circa 1877. Courtesy of the Concord Free Public Library.

TRUE GRIT

Louisa Alcott, "29 August—reading Little Women . . . 4 September—finished Little Women this eve." While the success of this work surprised its author, she conceded that "it reads better than I expected." It may well have been the reason for celebration at this time when Edward Damon escorted Louisa Alcott home at midnight from a party at his mother's house.

At a local meeting of the Farmers Club, Damon listened to Bronson Alcott's discourse on "Spiritual Horticulture," only to have the mood of the evening shattered—"smashed buggy on the return home." On 29 November 1879 Damon attended the party at Franklin Sanborn's home in honor of Bronson Alcott's eightieth birthday. One month later, on December thirtieth, Damon noted the tragic death of May Alcott Nieriker in Paris from complications of childbirth, and this time the gathering at Sanborn's was for her memorial service. There Sanborn described May's love of acting and her work in founding the local Shakespeare club.

A prodigious worker, Edward Damon nevertheless was often in delicate health, suffering from rheumatic pain and respiratory and digestive ailments. Chronic lung disease was given as the reason for his exemption from the draft in the Civil War. Slight in build, he recorded his weight "151¾ pounds after a big dinner meeting," and this never varied by more than a pound over the course of the diaries. His rheumatic condition eventually left him with a rigid knee and the removal of the elbow joint on his arthritic left arm, though doctors had advised amputation of the entire arm. Damon was almost sixty years old when he learned how to ride a bicycle. To Smith he exhibited "true grit and a quiet spirit."

Damon was not extreme in his views on temperance, according to Henry Smith, and enjoyed "a good cigar and an occasional glass of wine," though such departures from the ordinary were duly recorded in his diaries. Attending one temperance meeting, he observed that "a rather free and uncourteous discussion took place when the lecturer did not show." At one meeting the question was posed, "Which is calculated best to promote the cause of temperance—moral suasion or legal suasion." Damon advocated the legal position. A memorandum at the end of his 1869 diary includes a cure for drunkenness.

Sunday church services were both a morning and afternoon event, and Damon regularly attended the Trinitarian Congregational Church on Walden Street, where he was the superintendent of the Sunday school. His Sunday diary entries contain a record and sometimes a commentary of the sermons delivered. "Liked the afternoon sermon better than the morning but that is not saying much" [18 May 1862]. "A Mr. Willard from Andover preached a devilish poor sermon" [1880]. For many years he referred to his wife Anne's membership in the First Parish Unitarian Church as attendance in "the other church." As he grew older, Damon became more liberal in his religious views, frequently attending and contributing to "the other church." And it was the fiery orator and politically active Unitarian minister the Reverend Grindall Reynolds who presided at his funeral. Reynolds's influence in town extended beyond the pulpit that he preached from for twenty-three years. After attending a talk that Reynolds delivered on the Indian population, Damon commented on its excellence in his 1877 diary and recorded "100,000 civilized, 100,000 half-civilized and the remaining wandering." The following year a Dr. Barrows delivered a sermon at the Unitarian meeting house on the "3-fold belt of danger—Indians, immigrants, Mexicans." In addition to Sunday church services, evening prayer meetings were held at the mill. Damon was bothered when emergencies necessitated breaking the sabbath. When flooding at the mill made it necessary for him to work on Sunday, he wrote in his 1881 diary, "do not like to do work on Sunday—never did so much any Sunday before and hope never to as much again."

Damon's accounts were recorded "with scrupulous exactitude and his business books were kept with great accuracy," according to Smith. And with a strong sense of the work ethic, such entries frequently assess whether daily accomplishment measured up to expectation. Recorded as well was the wide range of books that he read with a special fondness for the enduring classics of Charles Dickens and William Shakespeare. Similarly, on a seven-month ocean voyage to Europe with his family in 1867, during a time when such trips were rare, Damon kept a detailed account of his travels through England, France, Italy, and Switzerland. Monarchs ruled the continent and accentuated the uniqueness of the American political experiment. At the Paris Exposition in July, he viewed the display of looms and shuttles of his craft but also found it significant to note, "saw a young lady smoking." In a contemplative mood he offered the self assessment: "I have my own views and am perfectly willing that others should enjoy theirs. I wish I was nearer what I try to be and hope when I return that I shall be able to manifest a better Christian life. . . ."

The family farm offered a welcome respite from the factory, and Damon found pleasure in the growth of his crops, proclaiming in one instance that a strawberry in his garden measured 8⅝ inches in circumference, which he then divided seven ways at the dinner table. He owned cattle, raised horses, and as an observer of the varying moods of nature was able to draw an appreciation for the moment. "It has been a damp cool day. The evening shadows were beautiful and there is a splendid aurora in the night . . . The sunset light was lovely and the clouds a beautiful rainbow, a bright starlight evening . . . Anne and I sat on the grass and saw the moon rise . . . As we came up Main Street in town the view of the western golden sky streaked with narrow clouds between the trees, was very singular and beautiful."

Smith reflected that his cousin "took a serious view of life but enjoyed fun and a good joke. He had a quick temper, which while at times manifesting itself, was well under control. If he said a harsh word unjustly, he was quick to make reparation. He never spent any money foolishly or cared for ostentatious display." As Smith concluded "it was a life lived plainly but well."

Genesis

The rapid flow of the Assabet River and final descent at Westvale before joining the Sudbury provided the base of power that brought the Damon Mill to its nineteenth-century commercial dominance.

The site's earliest industrial use dates back to 1658 when it was used to collect and forge peat bog iron ore for the Saugus Iron Works until the end of the seventeenth century. It was subsequently used as a grist mill, a fulling mill for the finishing of cloth woven at home, and in 1808 became one of the earliest cotton mills in the nation under the ownership of Ephraim Hartwell of New Ipswich, New Hampshire, and John Brown of Concord. They purchased the mill from Ezra and Lot Conant, whose family had owned it since 1714 when their grandfather Lot Conant Jr. purchased the property with Jonathan Herrick, both from the town of Beverly.

The house alongside the mill became known as the "1775 House". On the nineteenth of April according to lore, John Brown's father, Col. Roger Brown was having the frame of his house raised when the confrontation at the North Bridge took place and the workers laid down their tools to take up arms. The house was later acquired by Edward Damon along with other property belonging to the Brown family.

By 1830 Hartwell's nephew Ephraim Hartwell Bellows acquired the major interest in the five-story wooden mill which now had twenty looms and employed forty people. That year Bellows and Brown had a bitter dispute which attracted public attention when Bellows axed the main shaft made of wood and brought the mill to a standstill. While Brown won a lawsuit against his part-

Calvin Damon purchased the wooden mill
in 1834 and the following year developed a cotton
and wool flannel that became an American staple.
(Courtesy of the Damon family)

ner, Bellows had already sold the property on 14 April 1831 to Thomas Lord and Company, commission merchants in Boston. The property was again sold on 20 September 1833 to James Derby of Exeter, New Hampshire, for the manufacture of cotton and woolen machinery.

The Damon legacy began when Calvin Damon bought the mill for $18,000 on 26 December 1834. The purchase was assisted financially by his wife Rebecca's uncle James Johnson, the head of the Boston commission house of Johnson, Sewall, and Company, who became the mill's first selling agent. At the time Damon had been operating a woolen factory at the outlet of Lake Cochituate in the village of Saxonville and referred to both mills in a letter to his brother Benjamin on 5 April 1835. "I have a great pressure of business at this time; make about one hundred and twelve pieces of flannel per week at this place, and shall have my other factory started at Concord in the course of a few days; shall operate forty looms there in the course of the summer." A month later the Saxonville mill burned.

For Calvin Damon, born on 17 February 1803 in Amherst,New Hampshire, the road to Concord went back six generations with the arrival of thirteen-year-old John Damon in 1633 from Reading, England, as one of the first settlers of Reading,Massachusetts. One of the pioneer woolen manufacturers in New England, Abraham Marland was a mentor to the young Calvin Damon, who worked in his counting room at the Marland Mill in Andover, Massachusetts, and was a partner with his son John in Saxonville.

When they arrived in Concord, Calvin and Rebecca Damon lived on Water Street in the brick-end house and a home built next to it before purchasing the Rufus Holden farm across from the mill in 1839. The property passed to Edward when he married, was his home for most of his life, and continues to be owned by the Damon family.

While employed in the woolen mills at Andover and Saxonville, Calvin Damon became familiar with the manufacture of satinets, a fabric with a cotton warp and wool filling that was used by woolen manufacturers in New England to produce men's clothing. To make his mill competitive, Damon developed a fabric woven in the same manner as ordinary flannel, but with a cotton warp and wool filling. His new fabric had the merits of little shrinkage, was light and warm, and became a substitute for the "linsey-woolsey" undergarments manufactured at home. When he took a sample of the cloth to Boston and showed it to James Johnson, the story goes that the merchant animatedly responded, "Dom it, that is good cloth; it will sell"; and from that conversation the name *domet*, also spelled domett or dommet, was derived. The stonework at the mill that Calvin Damon placed along the tailrace and riverbank to contain erosion, still remains.

Calvin Damon's ledgers for the years 1835 through 1837 survive and give some indication of payment to the sixty-four workers, though the alternate use of surname initials with first names does not offer a consistent identifiable sample. Calvin Damon paid his operatives once a month, more frequently than the few times a year that prevailed at some mills, though it was unclear whether this was in cash, or as was common practice, credit for goods charged. No company store was known to have existed in Calvin Damon's time but each worker's account was debited with amounts "for sundry goods as per day book." Male weavers averaged $26 a month; female weavers, $16 a month.

Doffing. — The process of removing bobbins or cops from the spindles. — *Posselt.*

Doffing-Cylinder. — A carded cylinder in a carding-machine for removing fibers from the teeth of the main cylinder. — *Century.*

Doffing-Knife. — In a carding-machine, a steel blade with a finely toothed edge, which is reciprocated by a crank tangentially to the teeth of the doffer, for the purpose of taking from it the carded wool which is collected into a sliver. — *Century.*

Dog Wool. — See *Cottum.*

Doily. — (Said to be named from the first maker. *Doily* or *Doyley.*) 1. An old kind of woolen stuff. 2. A small ornamental napkin, often in colors, fringed and embroidered. Also spelled *doyley.* — *Century.*

Domeck. — An English name for an inferior grade of damask. — *Spitzli.*

Domestics. — Home-made cotton cloths, either bleached or unbleached of the grades in common use, and neither printed nor dyed. (United States.) — *Century.*

Domett. — A flannel cloth having a cotton warp, invented by Calvin C. Damon, at Concord, Mass., about 1834. It is said that the merchant to whom it was shown, having examined it carefully, exclaimed, "Dom it, that's good cloth," and that this was the origin of the name, which, slightly changed to *domet, domett,* or *dommet,* as it has been variously spelled, was at once given to the fabric. It shrinks but little in washing, and is well adapted for many of the purposes for which all-wool flannels are used.

Donskoi. — (Russian *Donskoï,* of the river Don.) A variety of Russian wool of coarse quality, first introduced into English woolen manufacture about 1830.

Doorea. — A variety of Dacca muslin of the finest quality, printed in colors, and striped. — *Century.*

Doosootee. — Cotton cloth used for tents and other things requiring strong material, from Agra, in northern India. Also *dosootee.* — *Century.*

Doria. — A cotton cloth woven with stripes of different thicknesses. — *Century.*

Dornick. — So called from *Dornick,* a town in Belgium, where this cloth was originally made. A similar cloth is said to have been made at Mornock, in Sutherlandshire, Scotland. 1. (Obsolete.) A stout linen cloth, especially a damask linen having a simple diaper pattern. 2. Linsey-woolsey: in this sense *darnick.* — *Halliwell.* Provincial English. — *Century.*

Dornock. — A term now generally used for checkered table-linen. The word has been spelt in many ways, — *dornix, darnex, dornex, darnec, darness,* etc. It would appear that it had a double significance, for dornock is said to have been a coarse description of damask, wrought at Tournay (frequently called Dorneck), in Flanders. — *Beck.*

Dorsel. — (Obsolete.) A kind of woolen stuff.

Dorset, or **Dorset Horn Sheep.** — These sheep are found in the southwest of England, principally in the county of Dorset. They are very hardy and prolific. Of the intermediate wools, Dorset is clean, soft, and

An 1893 textile glossary included Calvin Damon's development of domet cloth. (Courtesy of the Museum of American Textile History)

The carders were men who averaged between $32 and $34 a month; while the card-tenders were children and included a boy who was paid $11.62 a month and a girl paid $8.52. The rotating wire-toothed cylinders of the carding engine further cleaned the cotton and wool after they left the picker and separated the fibers so they would lie parallel to one another without breaking. The card-tenders carried the cotton and wool to be placed in the carding engines and took care of cleanup and maintenance around the machines.

"Uncle" Jesse Willis, the machinist in whose repair shop Edward Damon and Henry Smith spent time during their school days, earned $1 a day. His service to the Damons was a lengthy one and his name appeared in the federal census and in local directories as employed by the Damons during the duration of their ownership. One entry in a 1834 ledger, while Calvin Damon was still in Framingham, showed that he paid himself $125 every three months. Many surnames are repeated indicating that members of the same family were employed, and as listed in Concord Births, Marriages, and Deaths, some workers married one another. On 27 October 1836, Sophia Snow a drawer and William Dunn a spinner were married by the Reverend Ralph Waldo Emerson.

A list remains of over one hundred book titles encompassing a range of subjects, some quite erudite, from the mill's "Factory Cooperative Lending Library," whose name suggests extended use beyond Damon's workers. One surviving book from the library on Massachusetts plant life, was numbered forty-three and includes the rules for borrowing and fines for overdue books, with all disputes to be settled by the library committee.

Related through their mothers, Edward Damon was three years younger than his cousin Henry Francis Smith. "As cousins who were very fond of each other, we frequently exchanged visits at my home in Bradford, Massachusetts and at our grandfather's at North Andover, sharing winter memories of long sleigh rides, buffalo robes, and footwarmers," remembered Smith. During the winter of 1846–1847, he lived with the Damons when he attended the Factory Village district school with Edward. They later roomed together at Lawrence Academy in Groton.

Meshed between school days, the mill was a favorite haunt of Edward's youth, from the counting room to the repairs of the machine shop where he learned the use of tools. "You want to know how I get along. I work in the cotton room tending drawing. It is very clean work for the factory. I go to work at seven and work half an hour, then half an hour for breakfast, then work again from eight o'clock until half-past twelve. Commence again at one o'clock and work until half-past seven. I like it very well," he wrote to his cousin Henry Smith on 29 January 1850 at age thirteen. Drawing the fibers involved twisting them into a roving strand that added strength and improved the uniformity. The four pairs of rollers of the drawing frame made the fibers more parallel and the resulting sliver longer. For this job a boy would generally be paid then $2.50 a week.

Henry Smith spent his youth learning the woolen manufacturing business and in 1853 worked for $18 a month at B. W. Gleason's woolen mill in Rock Bottom, a village of Stow, which gave him experience in a range of jobs from sorting and scouring wool to the finished product. His son Henry described him as "large in stature and strong in proportion," in contrast to the slight build and delicate health of his cousin Edward. "While serving on the Board of Selectmen," his son recalled that "he would not hesitate to curb rowdy citizens and would march such crestfallen disturbers of the peace to home or lockup whichever at the time seemed more suitable."

In the spring of 1852 Edward Damon's formal education ended at Phillips Academy, Andover, when he returned to the mill and counting room to keep his father's accounts. It was an experience which served him well for at age 17½ he was thrust in the position of leadership upon his father's death of pleurisy on 12 January 1854 at age fifty-one. It was "a cold day with heavy snow for the funeral," Henry Smith remembered. "It was a terrible blow for Edward under 18 years of age."

Fortunately, the mill had prospered and Calvin Damon's family of four sons and three daughters was left financially comfortable. Henry Smith noted that his uncle had "accumulated a smug little fortune for those days." Rebecca Damon initially considered moving permanently back to the family home in North Andover but decided to purchase the David Loring house on Main Street in Concord Center, today owned by Concord Academy, where she lived from 1857 until her death in 1882. Henry Smith recalled that "as long as she lived her house was one of the leading social centers in town where the young people were cordially welcomed and enjoyed her hospitality."

His future career course determined, Edward Damon assumed control of a mill which not only weathered the unsettled conditions of a nation bitterly divided by war, but expanded and diversified its operation. The year 1860 that brought forebodings of imminent war with the South was the year that Anne Hagar of Weston and Edward Damon were married. An unidentified diary, probably belonging to a family member, described the October 17 day as "warm with doors and windows open. Could not have been a pleasanter time for a wedding day. Anne was married at 12 o'clock. Wedding and entertainment went well."

The Blood of Brothers

Inscribed on the Soldiers Monument in Monument Square are the names of 43 Concord men who "died for their country in the War of the Rebellion." The impact of that war was directly felt in the Concord community through the 466 men who served.

Massachusetts senator Charles Sumner initially feared that economics would dictate a union between the northern mill owners and their southern suppliers. In a speech delivered in the Senate in 1848, Sumner expressed his fear of "an unholy union between the lords of the lash and the lords of the loom."

Within Concord, anti-slavery sentiment was strong and was the driving interest and crusade of Franklin Benjamin Sanborn. Edward Damon was present when Sanborn lectured on emancipation at the Lyceum. Variously referred to as educator, journalist, reformer, and philosopher, Sanborn ran a school at his Sudbury Road home. He joined Bronson Alcott, William Ellery Channing, Ralph Waldo Emerson, and Henry David Thoreau in forming the Concord Club for weekly conversations in members' homes and was the secretary of the Concord Town Committee to raise funds for the settlement of the border state of Kansas as free territory. Through the Massachusetts Free Soil Association, he worked to get money, arms, and supplies to Kansas free-soilers and he helped slaves escape. Sanborn sponsored fellow abolitionist John Brown in his appeals in Boston and Concord, for armaments necessary for the slave revolt he sought to lead. With this intent the raid of the federal arsenal by Brown and eighteen of his men took place at Harper's Ferry, Virginia, on 16 October 1859. When Brown was tried for treason and murder and hanged two months later, Franklin Sanborn was included in the Senate investigation of the incident.

Articles of Agreement made and entered into

this *Sixteenth* day of *August* Anno Domini one thousand eight hundred and *Sixty one* between *Maj D H Vinton*

Quarter-master, U. S. Army, of the first part, and *Edward C. Damon of Concord State of Massachusetts* of the second part.

This Agreement Witnesseth, that the said *Maj D H Vinton Lt M St Army* for and on behalf of the United States of America, and the said *Edward C. Damon*

for *himself his* heirs, executors and administrators, have covenanted and agreed, and by these presents do mutually covenant and agree, to and with each other, as follows, viz:

First—That the said *Edward C Damon party of the Second part* shall have manufactured and delivered at the UNITED STATES DEPOT OF ARMY CLOTHING AND EQUIPAGE, *cor* Howard and Mercer Sts., in New York city, by or before the *Sixteenth* day of *December* next, the following named articles, to wit:

Fifty thousand Yards of White Cotton and Wool Flannel thirty one inches wide weighing six and one half ounces per Yard

Second—It is agreed that all the above named articles shall be like and equal in all respects, as to shade of color, quality of material, pattern, workmanship, finish, &c., to the sealed standard samples, deposited in the Office of Army Clothing and Equipage, New York city, on which this contract is based.

Third—It is agreed that deliveries of the above-named articles shall and will be made within *twenty* days from and after the *16th* of *August* and that at least *one third* of the quantity herein contracted for, shall and will be delivered as above provided for, in equal monthly proportions, within *two* months from the *16th* of *August* 186*1* and the remainder within *two* months thereafter, in equal monthly proportions, or in greater quantities should the contractor find it convenient. In case of failure on the part of the party of the second part to deliver the articles within the time and in the manner specified in this agreement, the party of the first part is authorized to make good the deficiency by purchase in the open market, at the expense of the said party of the second part.

During the Civil War, the Damon Mill manufactured cloth for Union Army uniforms. This order on 16 August 1861 paid Edward Damon twenty-five cents for each yard of the white cotton and wool flannel cloth.
(Courtesy of the Damon family)

Accosted at the Concord Post Office in January 1860, Sanborn was handed a summons to appear in Washington to testify; when he did not, a warrant was issued for his arrest on April 3, citing him for contempt. Putting up a forceful struggle against the federal marshal and his two assistants who had come for him, Sanborn was dragged handcuffed from his home, while he kicked and literally shouted murder. The church bells rang rallying the townspeople, and a writ of habeas corpus by Associate Justice of the Supreme Judicial Court Ebenezer Rockwood Hoar, later appointed Attorney General in Ulysses Grant's cabinet, resulted in Sanborn's release the next day in the Massachusetts Supreme Court.

On 19 April 1861 the Concord Artillery received orders to join the Fifth Massachusetts Regiment in Boston to go to the nation's capital, then in danger of capture by the rebels. On that day the Sixth Massachusetts Regiment, which included many mill workers from Lowell, were enroute to Washington when they were attacked by mobs in Baltimore. The following week, the Merrimack Manufacturing Company optimistically predicted that the war would be a short one and ample profits could be realized from the resale of raw cotton inventories at inflated war prices to other New England mills. Their decision was to reduce cloth production and discontinue it four months later. The Lowell mills, owned by a small circle of interlocking directorates, known as the Boston Associates, followed the Merrimack Company's lead, a decision that historians would call a "stupendous blunder." Lowell lawyer, historical writer, and corporate reformer Charles Cowley, expressed outrage at the consequences. "The impartial historian cannot ignore the fact, painful as it is, that nine of the great corporations of Lowell, under a mistaken belief that they could not run their mills at a profit during the war, unanimously, in cold blood, dismissed 10,000 operatives, penniless into the streets." The mill girls returned to the farms of New Hampshire and Vermont, their boarding houses closed and later sold; and when the war ended an immigrant labor force took their place. In nearby Lawrence, however, mill owners reasoned that the war would be long, and well supplied cotton inventories meant profitable war contracts. The woolen industry benefitted from contracts for army clothing and blankets.

Overleaf: One of the earliest photos of the center of town. The private residences are gone but several of the business structures still remain.
Circa 1865. (Courtesy of Richard W. Spaulding)

The demand for manufactured cloth stimulated by the war was filled by the increased output made possible with the prevalence of the power loom by 1850. One person could tend three or four looms with an output of ninety to one hundred sixty yards of cloth a day, in contrast to home woven cloth that produced only four yards daily.

During the war the Damon Mill turned out cloth for the uniforms of the Union Army. The war brought prosperity as well to Amory Maynard's Assabet Manufacturing Company, which supplied the army with woolens, flannels, and blankets. Frequent trips by train to the Boston Cotton Exchange and entries that read "received a lot of cotton today," show Damon experienced no difficulty in securing supplies. The range of probable suppliers includes conquered southern territory, seizure from the blockade, Egypt, India, and Brazil, rerouting from ports like Liverpool, England, after shipment arrived from the South, and in the early stages of the war, from Lowell. The price of cotton rose during the war from $.11 to $1.67 a pound, and many factories, as in Lawrence, switched to the manufacture of woolen goods.

In May 1862 Damon went to Faneuil Hall to see the Concord Company, and Anne attended Soldiers Aid Society meetings to raise money on their behalf. News of the capture of New Orleans and the destruction of the Confederate ironclad warship the *Merrimack* pale in importance to the loss of his brother Willie. Corp. William Damon of the First Battalion Infantry, Massachusetts Volunteers, died of fever at Harrison's Landing, Virginia, on August 5. The disciplined writing style abandoned in the space normally reserved for the crowded account of the day, an anguished Edward Damon boldly scrawled: "Willie is dead. God is love. Infinite wisdom orders all events. Have no heart for business—everything that would have given me pleasure now adds to my sorrow." The day before he wrote of local enthusiasm to volunteer in the war effort that extended to his factory workers. "All my men have been off this afternoon—great excitement about enlistments."

Damon himself was exempted from the draft because of chronic lung disease. He remained sensitive to the cost of human loss in measuring military success. On 15 December 1862 he wrote, "The news from Fredericksburg shows terrible loss from battle even if we obtain the victory." While his diaries refer to "grand receptions" for returning regiments, they mention as well community feeling when life was lost, as on 9 August 1863, "Francis Buttrick wounded at Gettysburg, buried under arms this p.m.—very large funeral procession."

In the 1863 Annual Report, Selectmen Addison Fay, Nathan Stow, and Elijah Wood condemned the southern rebellion which they viewed as treasonous. "The God in Heaven never looked down upon a more wicked, unjust and diabolical set of scoundrels than those now carrying on this Slaveholders Rebellion. It was conceived in inequity and brought forth in sin. It is swallowing up the blood of thousands of the noblest men in our land. It is carrying desolation into almost every household. It lays its bloody hand upon almost every family. It proposes to destroy the best earthly government, and to erect upon its ruins the vilest. . . .

"This war found this town with an established reputation. That reputation we propose to maintain. Whatever we are called upon to do, whatever sacrifices we are called upon to make, in carrying this war to a successful termination, that we will do—that we will make. We look to no result short of success. . . ."

When word of Gen. Robert E. Lee's surrender came on 10 April 1865, Edward Damon was "ploughing a lot of land in the cow pasture." His relief that the divisive fighting was over and the nation's unity restored was numbed by the fatal shooting of Pres. Abraham Lincoln and the wounding of Sec. of State William Seward. On April 15 he wrote in his diary, "the startling and terrible news of the assassination of the President and attempt to kill Seward came this morning filling all hearts with grief and gloom." The mill bell tolled for an hour on the nineteenth of April in memory of a beloved and fallen leader.

Subsequent Memorial Day celebrations honored the Civil War dead and the surviving veterans. The Damon Mill was closed for the holiday. "Did not run the mill because of Decoration Day," wrote Damon on 30 May 1870. "We decorated 16 graves. The Davis Guards and Assabet GAR met us at the monument as we returned. They came through here on the way home and we gave them lemonade, crackers, and cheese."

The Melvin Memorial in Sleepy Hollow Cemetery was carved by Daniel Chester French in tribute to the three fallen Melvin brothers—Asa, John, and Samuel, who lived off of Lowell Road, where Lindsay Pond Road is today. "In memory of three brothers born in Concord who as private soldiers gave their lives in the war to save the country. This memorial is placed here by their surviving brother [James] himself a private soldier in the same war." Asa Heald Melvin was killed in battle before Petersburg, Virginia, on 16 June 1864; John Heald Melvin died in a military hospital at Fort Albany, Virginia, on 13 October 1863; and Samuel Melvin, taken prisoner at Harriss Farm, Virginia on 19 May 1864, died at the infamous Andersonville prison in Georgia during September 1864. Ralph Waldo Emerson paid tribute to the youthful soldier of uncertain fate:

> So nigh is grandeur to our dust
> So near is God to Man
> When Duty whispers low "Thou must"
> the youth replies "I can."
>
> ("Voluntaries III")

Centennial

Commemorating the nation's one hundreth birthday in 1876, the Centennial Exposition in Philadelphia was a show of pride in industrial progress that included machine loomed fabrics. Prominent in the display at Machinery Hall was the Corliss steam engine, symbolic of America's technological capability.

Concord was a town of 2,676 people in March 1874 when Edward Damon became a member of the centennial committee of thirty to prepare for the celebration of the 19 April 1775 Concord fight, and the arrival of Pres. Ulysses S. Grant. Damon favored inviting Lexington for a joint celebration. The committee wrote a letter to the Concord Board of Selectmen in November 1873 suggesting that option. "Attended the meeting of centennial committee and fired the last shot for Lexington." The decision was left to Town Meeting which turned the invitation down in March 1874. The centennial committee favored the construction of an ornate bridge of cedar with the bark on and two arbor seating areas mid-way across, far different from the simple appearance of the North Bridge at the time of the Revolution, known through the 1775 engravings of Amos Doolittle.

It was at the centennial celebration that the seventy-two year old Emerson in a weak voice barely audible to the crowd delivered a powerful message. "We have no need to magnify the facts. Only two of our men were killed at the bridge, and four others wounded. But here the British army was first confronted and driven back; and if only two men, or only one man had been slain, it was the first victory. The thunderbolt falls on an inch of ground; but the light of it fills the horizon."

Through the efforts of Ebenezer Rockwood Hoar, who had served in Ulysses Grant's cabinet as Attorney General and was a member of the House of Rep-

Guests at Concord's 1875 centennial celebration. Pres. Ulysses S. Grant and his cabinet stand in front of the Main Street home of Judge Ebenezer Rockwood Hoar. Left to right: Vice-Pres. Henry Wilson, Pres. Grant, Sec. of War William Belknap, Sec. of State Hamilton Fish, Sec. of Navy George Robeson, Sec. of Interior Columbus Delano, Postmaster General Marshall Jewell. (Courtesy of the Concord Free Public Library)

Visitors to Concord's centennial walked across an ornate bridge of cedar, a contrast to the
simple appearance of the North Bridge at the time of
the American Revolution. (Courtesy of the Concord Free Public Library)

resentatives, Congress donated ten pieces of condemned brass cannon for the casting of the Minute Man statue. The full-size plaster model made by the twenty-five-year old Daniel Chester French depicting the Minute Man who left his plow to grab his gun, was cast at the Ames Manufacturing Company in Chicopee, Massachusetts, and fulfilling the bequest of Ebenezer Hubbard placed on land on the west side of the river at the battleground. When the Social Circle opened its 1875 season that October, "the subject of renumeration of Dan French was discussed." Town Meeting in 1876 voted to pay French one thousand dollars for his enduring centennial legacy and Damon was one of the guests at John Keyes lawn party in honor of French, "everybody there and splendid time." A note of irreverance was recorded by Damon on 9 August 1875, "three boys are in the lockup for stoning the Minute Man."

"Anne, William and I saw the 'Minute Man' which was put on pedestal this morning. Think the pedestal should have had the date towards the bridge," Damon wrote on April first. On Patriots Day, "Anne and I drove about to see the decorations. Ralph and I went to the ball for an hour. It was a brilliant affair." But the long-awaited centennial could not be savored by the Damons as they kept the vigil for two-year-old daughter Rebekah, "so weak and sick. It is painful to be in the room," observed Damon of his infant daughter's respiratory struggle. "Dr. Cook and Mrs. Hosmer summoned. Bessie died at 11¾ o'clock," he wrote on 26 April. Two days later Rebekah Cotton born 15 June 1872, was buried at Sleepy Hollow Cemetery. "The earth at the grave was covered with evergreen and sprinkled with flowers. We laid dear little Bessie's body in the grave at the top of the hill and I remained till it was filled and decorated." Thereafter the grieving father paid a number of visits to "little Bessie's grave," and that November, "went to Lowell and ordered tablet for Bessie—$35."

Afterwards the Damons looked to Louisa Alcott's centennial scrapbook for an account of the celebration events they had missed. Damon was present in June at a reception for Gen. William Tecumseh Sherman's visit to Concord and the following month went to Boston with Judge John Keyes to select a commemorative fountain in Monument Square that was erected in August. "Had a good laugh on Judge Keyes finding the center of triangle for location of fountain."

The recurring explosions of the gun powder mills, located a mile to the west of Damon's mill, and the human loss that it exacted was now listed as a separate cause of death in the Town Reports. When Addison Fay, the general manager of the Massachussets Powder Mills which later became the American Powder Mills, lost his life in March 1873, Edward Damon was one of the pallbearers.

At his mill, Damon could hear the explosions. "Powder Mill blew up at 11:10 and Mr. Taylor was so terribly burned that he died before five."[5 September 1873] "Dr. Cook called to see me on his way home from the Powder Mills. At 8:10 two Powder Mills blew up one after the other and in 2 minutes 4 more. Keith was killed and Drew died at noon." [24 July 1877] "Powder Mills blew up killing Charles Perry. I was standing talking with Puffer at the time in front of W.D. Brown's house—It was the sharpest report I ever heard—it knocked bricks off the chimney of Brown's little house and threw down dishes in our house." [3 November 1877] The day that began with such turbulence ended for Damon with celestial serenity. "Mars and Saturn almost touch, Venus and Jupiter in South met—very beautiful."

Women still couldn't vote at Town Meeting for its nine school committee members in 1876 when Anne Damon was elected to the school committee. Concord's appropriation for all the schools then was $8,500, and the high school was just two small rooms in the town house with thirty-five pupils. The community was divided into district schools, and teachers were usually young women who had to cope with a wide range of ages among the students. Nor was there free suffrage when a poll tax could deter the poor from voting. On 31 October 1879 Edward Damon noted that the number of poll tax payers in Concord was 853. The following year when women were permitted to vote at town meeting, a disappointed Louisa May Alcott noted their poor showing. While the American democratic experiment was celebrated at home, the world was mostly governed by absolute monarchs. "An attempt was made on the life of the Czar yesterday," Damon recorded on 15 April 1879.

A favored recreation by the end of the century, baseball came to Concord in 1867 and initially the games took place at the cattle show grounds. In August of that year Damon wrote: "Sam Hoar came up to present the challenge of the Middlesex Club to the Union Club, which was played this afternoon. The

---

Overleaf: The north side of the Milldam facing Monument Square at the Concord National Bank of which Edward Damon became president. Circa 1880.
(Courtesy of the Terry McHugh Memorial Fund)

Baseball was introduced following the Civil War and town team rivalries
drew enthusiastic crowds. 1889. (Courtesy of Richard W. Spaulding)

Middlesex Club beating, though our club made a good show." The results of
a Saturday afternoon game in 1875 between Acton and Concord—"Acton beat.
Stow played with our boys this afternoon—our boys beat." There is also mention of a late autumn game of football in the centennial year. "The men and
boys had a fine game of football," he recorded on November 25.

On a summer's evening Walden Pond offered a retreat. "Had a fine moonlight
row on Walden—just a dozen of us—delightful evening." Walden was the setting for both temperance rallies and drunken disturbances. On 4 July 1879,
five thousand people were present to hear the prohibition oratory of Henry
Ward Beecher. Two years later there were reports of "drunken groups at Walden
invading the village and a large cache of beer found at the prison." The
unlicensed sale of liquor was a town problem during the centennial year.
"Frank Dowd was convicted of selling liquor. Sentenced 60 days and $50 fine—
appealed," noted Damon on 8 February 1876.

Town Meeting debated whether to issue liquor licenses and reflected the growing strength of the temperance movement. At times the vote was close as in 1881 when the advocates of licensing won seventy-eight to seventy-seven and selectmen issued the licenses to the two drugstores and the Middlesex Hotel. The following year Louisa Alcott's newly organized militant Woman's Christian Temperance Union made their presence felt at Town Meeting, and with their newly won suffrage the vote of 149 to 59 was a decisive no against licensing.

Boating was a popular recreation and many families had their own canoes. The festive Carnival of Boats procession held on the evening of July Fourth along the Concord River attracted eight thousand people in 1879, many of whom came to view the parade, hear the band's music, and see the sky ablaze with fireworks at the North Bridge. The state prison which opened in 1878 became a popular stop along the boating route, with the Damon family among the curious onlookers. That year the family's celebration began the evening of July third with a band concert at Warner's Hall on Commonwealth Avenue that belonged to Ralph Warner, owner of the wooden Pail Factory. The next day "we saw the regatta, went to Egg Rock and had a most delightful picnic. We went up river so we could see the prison." Just two weeks later Damon responded to the call for assistance in putting out the fire at the prison. "At 3:45 A.M. was awakened by the cry of fire. The shops at the prison were burned."

As a Water Board Commissioner Damon was responsible for working out the new prison's access to the town's water supply. "Water board went to the prison and saw the warden. While we were there two convicts got up on the roof and one was shot in the left side." After several meetings the Water Board voted to supply 200,000 gallons per day to the prison at a cost of $3,000 for a ten-year-period. Nine hydrants were installed in the prison yard and three on Commonwealth Avenue adjacent to the prison. The interest of the Damons in the prison extended beyond the curious. Edward Damon on occasion attended church services there and Anne visited the vocational shops.

The cattle show was an annual popular event in September that was regularly attended by Damon and his family. "Went to the cattle show this afternoon and saw the trotting which was pretty good. Show of fruit and vegetables was very fine and a large collection of cattle . . . Took Ralph and the girls to cattle show—dined in tent, fine show." Accommodations are made for his

Walden was a popular stop along the railroad. The pavilion built by the Fitchburg division
of the Boston and Maine railroad, attracted excursion trains to Concord.
There was a dance hall, bathhouses, boats to rent, and a racetrack.
Circa 1880. (Courtesy of the Terry McHugh Memorial Fund)

Overleaf: The cattle show was an annual September event that the Damons regularly attended.
Harness racing was included on grounds that are now Belknap and Elsinore streets.
Circa 1885. (Courtesy of Virginia Tucker)

FITCHBURG RAILROAD.

MIDDLESEX COUNTY

CATTLE SHOW

AT CONCORD, MASS.,

TUESDAY & WEDNESDAY, SEPT. 29 & 30, 1874.

Reduction of Fare!

EXTRA TRAIN FROM BOSTON.

Trains leave Boston for Concord at 6.15, (7.30 Express,) (8.45 Extra stopping at all stations and connecting at Waltham with train over Watertown Branch, leaving Boston at 8.30,) (10.50 Accom. to Waltham,) (11.10 Express to Waltham,) A. M., 2.15, (2.45 Express, stopping only at Waltham and Lincoln,) (3.55 Accom. to Waltham,) (4.15 Express to Waltham,) (5.30 Express,) 6 P.M.

RETURNING.

Leave Concord for Boston at 7.00, (7.52 Express,) (8.40 Express from Waltham,) (9.36 Express from Waltham,) 10.34 A. M., (1.30 Express from Waltham,) (5.00 Extra, stopping at all stations and connecting at Waltham with train over Watertown Branch, leaving Waltham at 6.10,) 5.40, 6.35 P. M.

FOR FITCHBURG AND INTERMEDIATE STATIONS, except Lunenburg, at 7.16, 11.59 A.M., 3.32, 5.07, 6.15 P.M.

FOR LUNENBURG at 7.16 A.M., 3.32, 5.07 P.M.

FOR MARLBORO' AND INTERMEDIATE STATIONS, at 8.10 A.M., 3.32, 6.15 P.M.

FOR STATIONS ON FRAMINGHAM & LOWELL, WORCESTER & NASHUA, AND STONY BROOK R. R.'s, at 7.16 A. M., 5.07 P. M.

For Mason Village and Intermediate Stations, at 8.10 A. M., 5.07 P.M.

For Stations on Nashua, Acton & Boston R. R., at 8.10 A.M., 3.15, 6.15 P.M.

Tickets for the Round Trip from Boston, Cambridge, and Belmont, 90 cts.; Waverley, 75 cts.; Waltham, 60 cts.; Stony Brook, 45 cts.; Lincoln, 25 cts.; Concord Junct., 15 cts.; South Acton, 30 cts.; West Acton, 45 cts.; Littleton, 65 cts.; Ayer Junct., 80 cts.; Maynard, 40 cts.; Rockbotton, 60 cts.; Hudson, 70 cts.; Marlboro', 75 cts.

☞Passengers who fail to provide themselves with Excursion Tickets before entering the cars, will be charged Regular Fare.

C. L. HEYWOOD, Sup't.

BOSTON. SEPT. 24th. 1874.

Accessible by train, the cattle show attracted wide area interest. (Courtesy of Peanut Macone) workers. "Have only run part of the mill today to allow those who wished to attend the cattle show," he wrote on 29 September 1875. The arrival of Barnum's circus was also a sought after attraction. While at times the town offered its own unexpected liveliness: "Had a great row on the Milldam this evening. Several men stabbed." On 3 October 1875: "Town had horse and buggy stolen last evening. Caught the man."

Responsive to the care of the needy, Edward Damon was among the members of the 1871 almshouse committee which designed and supervised the building of a new almshouse on the Walden Street site donated by resident Hugh Cargill. That same year there was local concern and participation by the Damons to help the victims of the Chicago fire. "The great fire in Chicago has cast a gloom over the whole country," Damon wrote in October 1871. "Been to town with Anne collecting for Chicago." Many references pertain to Anne Damon's work with the Female Charitable Society which in the next century evolved into the Concord Family Service.

When the town library moved from its courthouse quarters and opened its doors on 1 October 1873 at the intersection of Sudbury Road and Main Street as the Concord Free Public Library with over 11,000 volumes in place, Henry Francis Smith as selectman and library trustee delivered the opening address, and Edward Carver Damon and Ralph Waldo Emerson were among those who served on the library committee. The trustees were to be responsible for the building and endowment, but daily operations were under the library committee, then elected. The library's founder, William Munroe, who had prospered through investments made in the Pacific Mills of Lawrence, donated $1,250 for the purchase of reference books and offered another $1,250 if an equal sum were raised. Edward Damon and his mother Rebecca responded as financial contributors and book donors. In 1874 Damon gave 45 books to the library and his mother gave 33.

The 1875 library committee report complained that the collection had "too much fiction and too little of what may be considered the more solid and instructive works of the day." Realistically the report said that "the committee cannot decide what books the people shall read anymore than what they shall eat." But its six members nevertheless felt they could "exhibit some taste and some judgment and have some influence in regard to what goes on the bookshelves." That year Sophia Thoreau deposited the unpublished manuscripts of her brother Henry in the iron safe of the library under Emerson's trustee-

July Fourth parade down Main Street towards Monument Square.
A billboard advertises a show of the "Wild West." 1894.
(Courtesy of Francis Magurn)

ship. The library committee noted that they filled three trunks or boxes, and along with forty or fifty books of memoranda of the natural history of Concord and the Indians who lived here, included "a complete survey of almost every farm in town, which will be of great value in the future in regard to the boundary lines of different estates, especially so when we consider the established accuracy of Mr. Thoreau's surveys and measurements."

On 3 December 1874 school, church, and courthouse bells sounded the news that pure water flowed to Concord from the Sandy Pond reservoir in Lincoln through six miles of pipe laid. That effort was directed by the town's three elected Water Commissioners, one of whom was Edward Damon, and guided by the engineering advice of twenty-three year old William Wheeler. On December second Henry Smith wrote, "this morning went to the pond at Lincoln to let the water into the pipes" and triumphantly the following day, "drew Sandy Pond water in my house for the first time."

Independence Day was a holiday of firecrackers and hell raising for local

The tempo was spirited, the mood playful and irreverent as this turn of the century
July 4th parade makes its way along the Milldam.
[Courtesy of Virginia Tucker]

youth that began in the early morning hours and often strained patience. The
day before Damon gave warning to his workers, "told the boys and men that
any who made any noise before 5 o'clock tomorrow would do no more work
for me." They complied and 4 July 1879 proceeded peacefully. "There was no
noise till 5. We all went down to Town Hall at 8:30 A.M. and had music, a
short and fine address from Judge Hoar, and reading of the Declaration of
Independence by Mr. Emerson. We all went to the carnival of boats which was
a grand spectacle—about 40 boats. Got home at half past ten." "Helped Ralph
fire some crackers and burnt my fingers," Damon wrote in 1871 when Ralph
was eleven years old. The following day some of his workers were still on
holiday. "Have been rather short of help as a good many have not yet gotten
over the Fourth." White Pond was a favorite picnic and boating area. "We all
went to White Pond, joined with mothers family—a nice picnic. Anne got lost
going over Regatta and tub race at Flint's bridge." For the centennial year,
"the Antiques and Horribles Show was large and ludicrous in the extreme.

Went to town to see boat races, foot races and greased pole competition. Judge Keyes gave the historical address. Square fully lighted—fireworks."

Though still a workday, the celebration of Christmas began in New England in the years following the Civil War and in 1867 monies were solicited in Concord for a public Christmas tree, and in local homes, including that of the Damons, children were beginning to receive simple hand-made presents. In 1866 Damon referred to the "very large and pleasant gathering" around the Christmas tree at the schoolhouse. The following year he described a "white Christmas" festival at the schoolhouse on Christmas eve and a Christmas tree at the Trinitarian Church Sunday School. But it was not yet a holiday from work, for on the same day the "underfloor was laid on the new section of the mill."

Gifts exchanged were basic and simple. "Mother gave Anne a dozen tea-spoons and me some handkerchiefs," he wrote in 1869; "Smith brought a thermometer to Anne." The following Christmas, "the children have a tree," and two years later, "the children have a merry time with their presents." But for Damon it was, "been about the mill all day." In 1873 Damon worked during the morning and then visited his mother on Main Street in Concord Center where the family had "a cold dinner. Mother gave Anne a shawl, me a glass dish and the children a number of presents." For the next two years Christmas Day was spent in the counting room, but in 1876 Christmas ceased to be a workday for Damon. In 1878 the Damons gathered around their first family Christmas tree; the children's stockings hung in the sitting room while pre-dictably they were up early with anticipation to open presents and visit later in the day with relatives. The rhythm of Christmas had begun.

Been About the Mill All Day

[Another day like yesterday and troubles multiply. I feel like shutting up the mill and going 'a fishing. 17 May 1881]

Damon's mill was a highly visible presence within the surrounding village, creating a community within a community, but not in jarring discord with its pastoral nature. The descent of the water that turned the wheels and turbines was a self-renewing source of energy and a means of employment. Its owner was a manufacturer at the factory, but at home he raised crops and tended cattle on his farm.

Edward Damon's sense of responsibility extended beyond cloth production to the workers and surrounding village. Religious services, a lending library, adult education classes, and social events were available at the mill in the hall over the counting room. If Edward Damon was among the "lords of the loom," he did not function like the absentee corporate owners of the large mills of Lawrence and Lowell. The smaller family owned mill dictated otherwise.

From the bales of raw cotton and wool to its finished stage as cloth for dress goods, the entire manufacturing process took place on site. Moving among its pulley wheels, bevel gears, and horizontal and vertical shafts, Damon was involved in every aspect of mill activity, from sorting wool, carding, spinning, or finishing cloth, repairing machinery, balancing financial accounts, bailing water when the level rose too high, to the nasty job of cleaning out the wheel pits. "Went into wheels and found 2 eels under our gate. It took me nearly an hour and I could hardly stand when I came out" [1870]. "Have been at work on wheels most of the day—full of eels and leaves" [1871].

The battle against rising water seemed ongoing. "The water is fearfully high. It ran under the wool table and into the cellar. Spent all the morning trying to bank it up to stop it," he noted in this 1870 entry. "Had a hard job pumping out the wheel pit this morning. Just after dinner the water broke through and have the men working all night." But when the water level was too low, the mill's two turbine wheels and steam pump were idle. "The steam pump gave out at noon and Smith and I worked on it all the afternoon," read an 1869 entry, while a good performance was shown in the 1880 recording, " have run mill with engine alone for the first time and were able to keep up full speed with 70 pounds steam." Early spring was a particularly difficult time to cope with the rising water. On 26 March 1876 he wrote "the water is higher than I ever saw it before. It rained powerfully till 4 this morning. We have dykes all along the canal and in front of the woodsheds. Went to bed at 8 and slept 2 hours. Water in pond is above high water mark and 12 inches on finishing room floor." Three days later he was still working, having "spent the morning dumping stone into the hole between the bank and woodshed to prevent further washing." Efforts to erect a saw mill on 14 October 1869 were interrupted when "a man drowned himself in the canal and I talked with a man who was inclined to do the same." Though the task was completed by evening, the unforseen intervention of nature the following day forestalled any respite to savor the moment. When dawn broke, his diary announced without further explanation, "earthquake."

The Damon Mill, known also as the Damondale Mill, the Westvale Mills, and the Damon Manufacturing Company following a reorganization in 1889, was listed in the annual Blue Book Textile Directory as "manufacturers of cotton and woolen yarns, shaker and domett flannels, and all wool dress goods." Damon supervised quality control and monitored workmanship of an expanding line of cloth varieties that included berkshire shaker, excelsior shaker, convent cloth, carriage cloth, extra picklock, serge, all wool twill, and bedford cord. "Gave my opinion in reference to the cloth which was not up to my ideas and think the weaver and carder saw it in that light." Starting a new style of domett on 21 November 1877, he expressed dissatisfaction when the first run of cloth appeared, "a little too blue and the fine goods napped too much," and investigated further. "Made a special effort to discover the cause of spots of bluing that run in the pieces and think it is the flesh remaining on the wool or in the noils."

Winter meant coping with frozen pipes and exasperation. Damon could be found putting coal in the furnace to get the factory warm, examining cotton, or recording the hours of his workers, all before breakfast. "I have been in the counting room all afternoon and this evening," he wrote on 14 January 1864. "It is so late that I have decided not to go to the house and am going to take a nap on the cloth." The following evening he was called at 3 A.M. because, "the boiler exploded, fired up with no water in it." "We are about as miserable as we can be," he wrote on 12 January 1875.

He commented regularly about his own productivity with observations that range from "Had good speed today—made a full day—spent most of the day about the mill" to "another day like yesterday and troubles multiply. I feel like shutting up the mill and going 'a fishing'." Of all the areas of the mill, the counting room was Damon's special preserve and where he spent the most time. A sense of accomplishment was conveyed when he could say, "spent morning fixing cash book—made out pay envelopes this afternoon in 40 minutes and counted out money, checked payroll and balanced cash in an hour and 50 minutes making just two and a half hours pay off."

The diaries conveyed the arduous pace. "Took bath at factory midnight. Rose at 5:30." Gas lamps lit the mill often late into the evening. "Ran part of the mill till ten." "I have been putting up cloth most of the day and it was just five minutes of twelve when we got the last piece done." "I have worked hard not leaving the mill until after eight. There is not a dry thread in my shirts."

In 1859 Damon hired local surveyor Henry David Thoreau to prepare maps of the mill site. Thoreau advertised his business, "surveying of all kinds, according to the best methods known; the necessary data supplied in order that the boundaries of farms may be accurately described in deeds; woods lotted off distinctly and according to a regular plan; roads laid out, &c..&c." Thoreau was paid thirty-six dollars to survey the factory, outlying buildings, and workers' dwellings of the Damon Mill.

Thoreau resented the intrusiveness of industrial development on the rivers that powered its factories. "So completely emasculated and demoralized is our river that it is even made to observe the Christian Sabbath," he wrote in "The Rivers and the Sabbath." "On a Sunday morning the river runs lowest owing to the factory and mill gates being shut above. Not only the operative make the Sunday a day of rest, but the river too . . . The very rivers run with fuller streams on Monday morning. All nature begins to work with new impetuosity on Monday."

From May through July 1859, Thoreau recorded the surrounding flora,

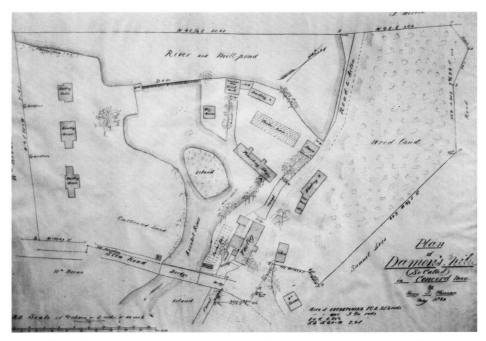

Henry David Thoreau was hired by Edward Damon to survey the mill in 1859.
One month after Thoreau's death, fire destroyed the wooden mill on 19 June 1862.
(Courtesy of the Damon family)

fauna, and insect life. "Hear the tea-lee of the white throat sparrow," he noted on May 6. "While surveying this forenoon behind Willis's house on the shore of the mill-pond, I saw remarkable swarms of that little fuzzy gnat (Tipulidoe) . . . Black suckers so called, are being speared at the factory bridge," and a week later, "bought a black sucker just speared at the factory dam, 15 inches long, blacker than I am used to, I think; at any rate a very good fish to eat, as I proved . . ." "Surveying Damon's farm and factory lot," he wrote on May 16. "Hear a tanager today and one was seen yesterday. Hear a bobolink and king-bird and find sparrows nests on the ground. At evening the first spark of a night hawk." Thoreau took a break while surveying to note the apple trees and rhodora in bloom and queried, "did I hear a bobolink this morning?" He de-scribed the Assabet River on July 21, "for about one-third the way from the factory dam to the powder mills the river is broad and deep, in short a mill-pond." Thoreau's death on 6 May 1862 preceded by one month the destruction by fire of the wooden mill he surveyed.

When the wooden mill burned on 19 June 1862 Damon was away on business in Lawrence, and Dr. Henry Barrett told him the news as he approached home. His reaction to the total devastation was stoic; and his resilience contrasted sharply with the outpouring of emotion when faced with personal loss. "It is a heavy loss but am not cast down, I have health and loved ones left. Have received many expressions of sympathy and good wishes and many came this eve." The very next day he began the long road back toward the construction of a new mill, using information gained from visits to other mills in Billerica, Lowell, Lawrence, Leicester, Haverhill, and Pepperill where he "looked about for some ideas." Settling insurance claims proved trying and apparently not to his satisfaction. "Insurance companies are a swindle, it is outrageous." Ever mindful of the danger of fire, he witnessed its destructive aftermath at other mills. "Went to see the Chase and Faulkner Mills which were burned yesterday," he wrote following a visit to Lowell in 1880. Damon and his mill employees actively manned Westvale's volunteer firefighting efforts, and their names are listed in the hook and ladder companies of the era's Town Reports. When a coat at the mill caught on fire, Damon was determined that the safety regulations posted in each room be observed "to the letter."

Rebuilding the mill took two years "of anxious thought and work and took its toll on his strength," remarked Henry Smith, who joined his cousin Edward as a partner at the end of that time. Eldridge Boyden, who had designed Mechanics Hall in his native Worcester five years earlier, was hired to be the architect for the new mill. Lumber was purchased in Lowell; bricks were bought in Shirley. "Brick is getting scarce—took freight train to Groton and then travelled to Shirley to hurry them along. Went to South Acton and not finding any brick kept on to Still River." Recounting a trip to Lowell, he wrote: "At 7 A.M. started for Lowell with the horses. Rather hard travelling, but made pretty good time, about two hours each way."

Too often for every step forward in rebuilding, there seemed a slide backwards. "Mistake in plans. Must take out all stone that had been laid. It is a bad job putting in foundation on the river . . . Stones are so wet that the stone men went home this morning . . . The water got under the head gate at the canal and I have had to draw off the pond . . . It is a much more difficult and larger job than I expected to put in the foundation."

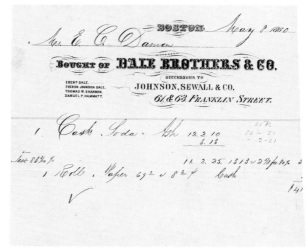

Eben Dale of Dale Brothers and Company. Portion of invoice from Dale Brothers & Co.
(Courtesy of the Damon Family)

When fire destroyed the wooden mill, Edward Damon immediately set about the task
of rebuilding. The granite tablet marks the construction of an expanded brick mill,
with increased production capabilities. 1986. (Photo by Alice Moulton)

BEEN ABOUT THE MILL

"Spent most of the morning on the steam pump—pumped out the wheel pit and this evening have had the back of the flume cemented and the wheel leveled up," he noted on 23 February 1863. But when the jack shaft came it wasn't right. "I shall in the future be careful how I allow others to make alterations in my plans." By March 6 he had progressed sufficiently to have "commenced white washing the mill." Five days later Damon went to Lowell to purchase tabletstones for the mill. "Put some coins and documents behind the date stone." And for luck, "nailed a horse shoe over the front door of the mill."

The rebuilding of the mill offered the opportunity for an expanded updated facility, and at this time Damon purchased the mill outright from other family members. The wooden mill was one hundred feet long and twenty-eight feet wide; the new mill measured one hundred five feet by fifty-two feet, with an ell thirty-by-thirty feet and three stories with basement and attic. It was a mill, observed Smith, "constructed in the most thorough and substantial fashion with reference not only to the essential requirements of the business but to architectural taste and proportions." The granite tablet with the name "Damondale" in raised letters set in the front wall united the names of Edward Damon and his selling agent Eben Dale of Dale Brothers and Company in Boston and New York. When the financial panic of 1873 forced Dale Brothers to settle for thirty-five cents on the dollar, the New York selling agents of Frederick Almy and Company, and then Converse, Stanton and Cullen, became their successors.

According to Henry Smith's memoirs, Damon originally expected his brother William to join him as a partner after his service in the army was over, an expectation that ended in August 1862 when at age twenty-one William died of fever during the Civil War. Another brother Benjamin was admitted as a partner in January 1866, but he died in November of that year at age twenty-three. When Henry Smith bought one-third interest in the mill on 1 May 1864, he already had fifteen years' experience in the flannel manufacturing business. The original domet cloth was diversified in the cotton yarns made for the warps and the different qualities of wool used for the filling. In addition some all wool flannel was manufactured. In 1865 the "Statistics of Certain Branches of Industry" listed for the Damon Mill the consumption of 40,000 pounds of cotton and the manufacturing of 566,000 yards of cloth valued at $216,000. Henry Smith's memoirs related "at the mill an average of 450 pounds of clean wool and 325 pounds of cotton were used daily to produce about 3000 yards of

On 2 April 1881, Edward Damon wrote in his diary "put two of the new Davis
and Furber looms into mill." 1883 loom catalogue photo.
(Courtesy of the Museum of American Textile History)

cloth per day including 'Damon's Original Domett' . . . The goods were very
popular and could be found in every part of the country and frequently copied
by other manufacturers." An 1890 edition of the History of Middlesex County
records one hundred fifty styles of goods manufactured, an annual product ex-
ceeding 30,000 pieces or 1,250,000 yards.

Trips by train to Boston were numerous to look over the cotton and wool
market and bid for purchase, though at times Damon left empty-handed.
"Looked about the cotton market and found it pretty stiff," or "went to Boston
at 9:02 and have done the wool market thoroughly but could not find the No. 1
I wanted." The very next trip on the 9:02 brought favorable results. "Purchased lot of wool of Robert Metcalf—straight 3/8 Missouri." He recorded with
satisfaction: "I looked around the wool market and think I got a good trade."
"Great excitement in Boston over sale of 250 bales of Dometts @25 cents,"
[1867]. "Bought 8 bales cotton of Hobbs @28 and offered 27¼ for 12 bales . . .

BEEN ABOUT THE MILL

Offered to make cotton yarn for 48 cents. We bought super wool for 84 cents" [1869].

Geographically, wool manufacturing was concentrated within the New England States. A lively business exchange existed between Damon Mill and the nearby Assabet Mills, manufacturers of blankets and flannels, in what became the town of Maynard. Founded by Amory Maynard and operated with his son Lorenzo, the Assabet Mills employed one thousand workers and became the largest manufacturer of woolen fabrics nationwide. "Sent some wool to Assabet to be colored" and "Mr. Maynard was down to see if we could make them some woolen yarn" were familiar entries. "Went to Assabet to see Maynard and told him we would spin five bales of cotton for him at 15 cents per lb. of yarn . . . Smith and I have been to Maynard's this afternoon. Agreed to let him have all the yarn we could make in September @72 cents plus tax" [1865].

Assabet was part of Sudbury until its incorporation in 1871 as the town of Maynard, so named in recognition of the prosperity and development to the area brought by the woolen mill and its founder. Powered by the same river source, the economic fortunes of both mills paralleled each other, the prosperity of the Civil War, the setbacks from the Depression of 1893 and the bankruptcy of both mills in 1898. Because Maynard was a company town, dependency on the mill was far greater than in Concord. The town had no banks and the five hundred Assabet workers generally deposited their savings with the company, almost half of which was reportedly lost. While the disillusioned and angry townspeople were contemplating changing the name of their town back to Assabet, a rebirth occurred the following year when the American Woolen Company bought the Assabet Mills and furthered its expansion. At this time, the American Woolen Company also purchased property in the Baker Avenue area and along Barrett's Mill Road, but decided instead to build the Wood Mill in Lawrence.

Henry Smith's son, Henry, Jr., recalled going to the mill to see his father in a poetic description that ignored the lint-filled air and the heat and humidity necessary to prevent the woolen threads from breaking. "I will remember my visits with him at the mill in Westvale and my interest in the activity there: the noise of the looms, the piles of snowy wool and whir of machinery in the carding and spinning rooms, the steamy atmosphere of the drying room and the queer odors of the scouring room, as well as the general mixture of colors in the dye house."

Bales of fleece to be cleaned and sorted at the Assabet Mills of Maynard.
Powered by the same river source, the Assabet and Damon mills shared similar
economic fortunes and a cooperative working relationship with one another.
[Courtesy of Ralph Sheridan and the Digital Equipment Corporation]

The twelve-year partnership with Smith was one of expanded production, the addition of new machinery, a dyehouse, and a brick building for the storage of stock and the sorting of wool. On 29 May 1865 Damon began making plans for a two-story addition to the mill. "Have spent a large part of the day thinking, marking, figuring and measuring about boilers and engines, but not being able to come to a decision" [1866]. "Spent whole day at new mill making calculations on wheels and gearing and got the saw mill raised" [1869]. Some old buildings were converted to tenement housing and new housing built. Repairs and modern woodworking machinery were under the supervision of Cyrus Fletcher of South Acton, whom Damon hired on 17 March 1873. "Talked with Cyrus Fletcher about working for us and looking after shop for a year and mentioned $100 per month and house rent beginning with first of October last which appeared to be highly satisfactory to him." Concord directory listings show that Fletcher remained in the employ of the Damon family throughout their ownership of the mill and developed his business beyond mill maintenance into construction work. A saw and grist mill operated on site and on 13 November 1869 Damon proudly recorded, "ground 100 pounds of meal in just 3 minutes, wheels are all we could wish." Located across the street from the mill was a grocery store for the workers, which according to Smith was "stocked with high quality goods and run at a low profit. All this was rendered necessary on account of the larger number of persons employed who would otherwise depend on teams of horses bringing provisions to the village two or three times a week."

As knitted garments replaced flannel for underwear, the mill adapted to making dress goods and cloth, but this was an expensive change, observed Smith. "Some of the expansion plans were no source of profit and proved to be an injudicious move." The partnership between the two cousins ended in December 1876 when Smith went into the wool brokerage business. It was a parting made difficult by their long association with one another. "Spent afternoon talking with Smith. I really feel worse for him than I have for myself in the darkest hour I have experienced," Damon wrote on 8 December 1876. Damon formed a new partnership with Edward P. Almy, then twenty-five years old, which lasted five years.

In 1889 the firm was reorganized as the Damon Manufacturing Company with Edward Damon as treasurer, his eldest son Ralph as president, and Charles Lincoln as mill superintendent. Ralph had gained experience working at the mill during the preceding decade, though not always meeting his father's expectation.

In an exchange of letters with Anne while on a trip to Maine during the summer of 1878, Edward Damon was annoyed at his seventeen-year-old son's lack of responsibility when filling in for the night watchman. At the same age he was in charge of the mill's entire operation. "I can only say in regard to not having steam enough, that excuses do not buy bread and butter and that the watchman's duty is to know whether he has supplies for his needs. It would have paid to have hired a man to work all night to get kindling. Ralph could have known at 6, 9, or even 10 o'clock if he could have been provided for." Concerned that her son might have fallen asleep while on duty, Anne Damon went to check on him, arriving at the mill "between 2 and 3 A.M."

A year before the nation-wide depression adversely impacted the mill's fortunes, the 1892 *Concord Directory and Guide* related the production of its "many styles of white dress goods, tennis cloths, and piece dyed goods. At present they are devoting their whole attention to the production of cloakings, dress goods, Bedford cords, worsteds, serges, etc., with New York City as the distributing center for the products." The mill and forty tenements were situated on twenty acres of land with power furnished by water wheels of one hundred twenty-five horsepower and a steam engine with the capacity of one hundred and seventy horse power. The capital stock of the company was listed at $120,000; the weekly payroll about $1,300; one hundred and seventy-five workers were employed when the mill ran at full capacity.

Concern and admonition for her husband's exhaustive workday were expressed in letters from Anne when he did take a vacation. Their growing family meant that he sometimes traveled alone and they wrote frequently to each other. His time away from home was never the issue; the pace of work was. "Don't mind the expense, it is well invested," Anne wrote to him in September 1878. " I hope you will stay as long as you can be contented. You know how quiet and uneventful the stream of life is in this neighborhood . . . It is important that you should relax the constant strain of business."

She chided him for "the folly of dashing along as you do," adding that "sometimes I think you live on a too stimulating diet—too much meat—and then rush and exhaust yourself. Friends not only powerless to prevent but are kept in constant state of self reproach because they do not keep up with you. I believe I am the only one who has made a stand and don't pretend to be smart nor accomplishing as much as I ought. I have no intention of lacing and chasing all my life."

Time away from the mill was needed. "When you are here you can't tell how you are, nor whether you are doing the work of one man or three. I think you are about the worst calculator of time for any given job and its probable extensions that I ever saw." She urged that he delegate more of the routine work to others and reserve his strength "for the emergencies of business. I am sure they are always coming. You will kill yourself at the rate you have gone on. You need a bookkeeper—thorough bred and high priced—not a half trained country fellow like Potter—and the sooner you bring your mind to the fact, the better it will be for you.

"I am willing to be economical on myself, and if our rich friends will mind their own affairs, on the children; but as for any further attempt at running your business economically, all the saving to come out of you and Mr. Almy, I protest against it. I don't think you learned anything from the fact that your father died 30 years sooner than he need from overexertion, but if you do it yourself, I hope the next generation will have enough of their mother's inertia in them to go slower."

The only surviving cloth samples from Damon's factory are half-a-dozen swatches of finished dress goods that were part of a log book for the year 1891, which includes directions for their manufacture. Analyzed by Concord weaver Rosita Corey, they show the use of fine weight yarns, some sett at sixty threads per inch in the warp and woven with sixty, seventy, eighty, or ninety picks (threads) per inch in the weft. Most of the fabrics described in the same log and entered for the year 1881 were sett in the range of thirty-six to forty-four threads per inch and woven at about the same per inch as with the all-wool carriage and twilled cloth.

A Show of Children

. . . Come now from Barrett's mill, Bateman's blue water,
    Nine Acre Corner, the Centre and all;
    Come from the Factory, the North and East Quarter,
    For here is a Union that never need fall;
        Lads in your blithest moods,
        Maids in your pretty snoods,
    Come from all homes that stand in our border;
        Concord shall many a day
        Tell of the fair array
    When young America met in good order.

[Song, "All the Blue Bonnets are over the Border."
from School Exhibition at Town Hall, 16 March 1861]

As Concord's school superintendent Bronson Alcott posed the challenge to his townsmen: "We spend much on our cattle and flower shows; let us each spring have a show of our children."

Alcott espoused a progressive pedagogy when he became school superintendent in May 1859 at an annual salary of $100. During his six-year term he conversed with students in a tireless effort to introduce them to the love of thinking. The most hopeful sign he saw appearing in the schools was that recitations were no longer just rote repetitions. Teachers were beginning to interpret the material, offering their own insights and encouraging students to express themselves in a conversational manner. He called for an end to the old-fashioned exercises of recitation that were "mostly sound and parrotry—a repeating by rote, not by heart, unmeaning sounds from the memory and no more."

The school committee to which Edward Damon was elected in 1862 included among its members such prominent town figures as Judge John Shepard Keyes, Franklin Sanborn, the Reverend Grindall Reynolds, and originator of the Concord grape, Ephraim Bull. The committee praised the efforts of Alcott's annual superintendent reports "to advance the true ideas of education" and recognized the influence of the classroom teacher. "The authority of the teacher has been so limited by public opinion that there is little danger of its becoming excessive; indeed one fault of all the children now growing up is that they are too little subjected to reasonable authority, at school and at home."

A high point of the school year was the exhibition held in March at which students from each school gave a public presentation of recitation and song. A program that remains of the school exhibition held Saturday, 16 March 1861, at Town Hall included the participation of Henry David Thoreau and Ralph Waldo Emerson in addition to remarks delivered by Superintendent Alcott. The program reflected concern for the preservation of the Union in the midst of civil war. The preparation that went into the Saturday annual event was aptly conveyed by Damon in this 15 March 1862 diary entry. "Exhibition went off finally—audience very large—hall packed. I am tired out."

His own schooling cut short by the demands of the mill and his father's death, Edward Damon remained a strong advocate of public education. His diary entries show that local educators, including Bronson Alcott, were guests at the Damon home. "The teachers Miss Fletcher and Miss Studley have been here this evening to read Shakespeare."

In a letter dated 30 August 1877 while on vacation in Maine, he wrote to Anne about the importance of education for the future of their son Ralph. "I hope that Ralph has made up his mind to study now and be at the upper end of his classes. If he wishes to go to college he must and if he does not he must that he may be ready in a few years to engage in business. I hope he will decide to go to college not for the name of it, but as a preparation for his life work."

The Concord school system then included eleven schools: three primary schools and the intermediate school and high school of the Centre district, which occupied rooms in the Town House, and the outlying district schools of the East Quarter, Nine Acre Corner, Factory Village, Barrett's Mill, Bateman's

---

Overleaf: School Superintendent Bronson Alcott, Ralph Waldo Emerson, and Henry David Thoreau, spoke to students and listened to their recitations at the 1861 spring exhibition of the Concord Public Schools. (Courtesy of Gladys Clark)

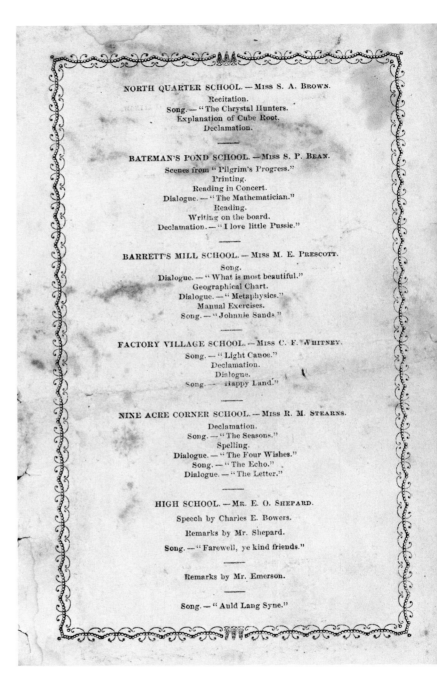

NORTH QUARTER SCHOOL. — Miss S. A. Brown.

Recitation.

Song. — "The Chrystal Hunters."

Explanation of Cube Root.

Declamation.

BATEMAN'S POND SCHOOL. — Miss S. P. Bean.

Scenes from "Pilgrim's Progress."

Printing.

Reading in Concert.

Dialogue. — "The Mathematician."

Reading.

Writing on the board.

Declamation. — "I love little Pussie."

BARRETT'S MILL SCHOOL. — Miss M. E. Prescott.

Song.

Dialogue. — "What is most beautiful."

Geographical Chart.

Dialogue. — "Metaphysics."

Manual Exercises.

Song. — "Johnnie Sands."

FACTORY VILLAGE SCHOOL. — Miss C. F. Whitney.

Song. — "Light Canoe."

Declamation.

Dialogue.

Song. — "Happy Land."

NINE ACRE CORNER SCHOOL. — Miss R. M. Stearns.

Declamation.

Song. — "The Seasons."

Spelling.

Dialogue. — "The Four Wishes."

Song. — "The Echo."

Dialogue. — "The Letter."

HIGH SCHOOL. — Mr. E. O. Shepard.

Speech by Charles E. Bowers.

Remarks by Mr. Shepard.

Song. — "Farewell, ye kind friends."

Remarks by Mr. Emerson.

Song. — "Auld Lang Syne."

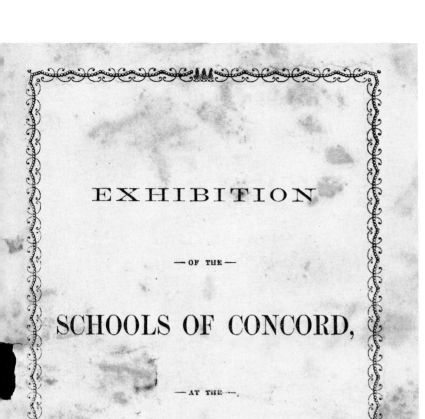

EXHIBITION

— OF THE —

SCHOOLS OF CONCORD,

— AT THE —.

TOWN HALL,

ON SATURDAY, MARCH 16th, 1861.

Pond, and the North Quarter. Alcott visited all the schools frequently and accompanied by school committee members administered examinations to the students.

Conscientious about his school committee service, Edward Damon noted the results of his visits. "Have been to examination of schools. In one particularly good in arithmetic but the reading was very bad" [3 March 1862]. "Examination very excellent. Mr. Alcott and Mr. Brown of the committee present" [17 November 1862]. Alcott maintained that such examinations "should deal more with principles than the text. A certain tenderness is becoming, seeing but not declaring too much. We must not put the victims under the compound blow-pipe of a consuming scrutiny, and search amid their ashes for any merits that may remain there to declare. We see blemishes soon enuf."

In Miss Jane Hosmer of the East Centre Primary School (located on a lot donated by the Emerson family opposite their home) Alcott found one such example of good teaching. "It has a mistress with a tact, almost a genius at pricking them forward as fast as one could wish . . . The drill mistress pins them for the time then relaxes to vary the performance; sometimes with a song, sometimes with a march, a little speaking, as the mood may require, the humor suggest."

Over fifty students ranging in age from four to seventeen were registered at the Westvale or Factory Village School, which made it the largest in town. It was hard to keep a teacher employed as school reports noted the "mixed sampling" of students, "some requiring a bit of restraint, and much given formerly to kicking against the pricks of authority."

The partnership of Edward Damon and Henry Smith assumed responsibility for the renovation of the school on land they donated at the corner of Main and Conant streets, and contributed to the cost of upkeep. The school committee was clearly pleased. In their report for the 1866–1867 school year they related that "in order to accommodate the fast increase in the population of Damondale, the schoolhouse in district No.4 was, by a vote of the town, passed last July, removed to a beautiful site nearer that village, on land presented to the town by the enterprising firm of Damon, Smith and Co. The schoolhouse was re-modelled, thoroughly repaired and is now the most convenient in this town."

Damon's sense of pride was apparent when examinations turned in a good report. In his 1871 diary he wrote "our school was examined this morning and

The children of Henry Francis Smith at their home on 61 Main Street.
The presence of tennis rackets reflect the interest of this era in the new sport.
Left to right: Henry F. Jr., B. Farnham, Theodore L., Wm. Lincoln, Herbert B.,
and G. Kirkham. Circa 1885. (Courtesy of the Concord Free Public Library)

it did itself and the teacher great credit." In 1872 Damon and Smith provided
a room at the school for adult evening classes, and four teachers were hired at
$1.50 a night.

Alcott's reports to the school committee offered his observations of the newly
arrived Irish as participants in the education experience. "Yankee blood first
deliberates, then aims carefully, sure to be mortified at missing its mark, but

---

Overleaf: The West Concord School opened in 1887 and replaced the Westvale District School,
no longer adequate to the area's population growth. The Harvey Wheeler School
built alongside it in 1918 responded to even greater population needs
and replaced the West Concord School. (Courtesy of the Damon family)

A SHOW OF CHILDREN

A SHOW OF CHILDREN 65

this foreigner shoots at the venture, hitting or not hitting, it matters not to him; so there is fire and the stroke . . . it is a stirring little bevy: the quick-witted Green-Islanders setting off to advantage the common sense of our children, acting as counterspurs and checks to one another, and working off contrast agreeable to witness. It must take at least a generation or more at this rate to blend the two peoples into one, and get off a nationality that America can fairly claim as hers."

State law in 1827 required all towns to establish free schools funded by public taxes. While attendance was made compulsory for some portion of the year in 1852, farm and factory work intruded. It was mandatory for children between the ages of five and fifteen years to attend school at least one term a year, and the town of Concord hired three truant officers to enforce this. Alcott sought community support by setting up Sunday evening meetings that engaged parents, teachers, and school committee members in dialogue about educational goals and stressed the importance of education in the home. Ambitious in scope these weekend gatherings were well attended.

Anne Damon was elected to the nine-member school committee in 1876, along with former teacher Abby Hosmer, four years before women in Concord were permitted to vote for the position at town meeting. They succeeded outgoing members Ellen Emerson, the first woman elected to the committee in 1870, and Henry Smith. Ellen Emerson and Anne Damon shared their mutual commitment to local public education. Damon's notation, "Anne attended the East Quarter School examination and dined at the Emerson's," is among the many diary references to his wife's leadership education role, her service a source of pride to him. Concerned that children who worked at Warner's Pail Factory along Commonwealth Avenue attend school, she went there herself "to see about scholars for the new school house." On 9 December 1879 Edward Damon wrote, "the school committee made some changes in the Center Schools—grading them which has stirred up a hornet's nest."

In 1880 Damon served on the committee to build the first high school which became the Ripley School on Stow Street. Further along the street the construction of the Emerson School in 1880 began the consolidation of primary schools in Concord Center. The new school attracted local attention and drew a Christmas Day visit that year from Ralph Damon and his sister Mary. The last remaining district schools closed in 1887. The year before, town meeting had appropriated $10,000 to build the West Concord School on Main Street to replace Westvale's district school. The town sold the old district school to Damon for $1,100, and the building is part of a private dwelling on Conant Street. Behind the new school, reflecting the growing popularity of tennis, the Nashoba Tennis Club was built. Among its board members was Edward Carver Damon.

To Give Good Long Days

John Welch agrees to work for me beginning tomorrow for $1.70 per day till December 1st. Work early & late—give good long days. [17 May 1871]

When the bell at Damon Mill rang a warning at 5:30 A.M. and again at 6:15 A.M., it signalled the beginning of a work day and a labor force that regularly included children. Child labor was a reality of life in the farms and the factories and Massachusetts led the way in its regulation with the enactment of the ten-hour day for women and children in 1874, a law taken seriously with enforcement provisions. Though Damon at times attended meetings with other mill owners, the only reference to the 1874 legislation does not reveal his position on the issue. "There was a meeting of employers at the Tremont House to protest against the ten hour bill. I did not attend it."

The federal census in Concord from 1860 to 1900 showed that entire families often worked in the mill and lived close-by. "Refused Sawyer goods at the store and he took his children out of the mill," Damon wrote in 1870, and the census for that year included six Sawyer girls ranging in age from eleven to twenty-two. During the latter part of the nineteenth century, the Westvale Mills included twenty rented tenements while houses and rooms to let were scarce. [The term tenement in this era meant multiple rental units and did not necessarily imply rundown housing.]

The age of children employed at Damon's mill rose accordingly with the passage of state regulation. By the 1880s and 1890s children of ages ten and eleven no longer appeared as mill workers in the local census when state law required minimum school attendance. "John White, state inspector made us a call. He was here, June 1879," wrote Damon. " All certificates must be authorized by school committee. The child under 14 must have attended school 100 days during the 12 months preceding the time at which he is working." Damon further recorded state regulations that required notice of working hours to be posted in each room and two ways of egress when five or more people were employed in any room above the second story, a safety measure with the danger of fire around flammable material.

The mill employed on average 100 workers, although the 1892 *Resident and Business Directory of Concord* stated 175. Workers were about evenly divided between men and women and between native born Yankees and those who arrived from Ireland; a smaller number of workers are listed in the census from Canada and Scotland. When commenting about his workers, the writings of Edward Damon never make a distinction between the native born and those of Irish descent during an era when the newly arrived Irish were subject to deprecatory remarks. Little continuity in the work force was evident from one ten-year census to another, reflecting a mobility common among textile mill workers and the nation's labor force in general. Mobility and change were part of the American way in an expansionist era, reflecting the freedom of its workers to move on in an attempt at self improvement. Today, while the family of Edward Damon live in Concord, there are no known families descended from his mill workers.

Damon donated the site for a schoolhouse close to the mill and was involved in the expense of its upkeep. When one of his young workers in 1879 proved troublesome at school, Damon threatened not to employ him. "Maurice Coughlin was sent home from school. I told him he could not have work until he had a certificate of good behavior from his teacher." But Coughlin proved to be a difficult employee and was dismissed two years later. "Informed that some of the boys were making a great deal of noise about the store. Told Maurice Coughlin to go home and not to come to work again. Gave a number of boys and men their notice." The next day he was angrier. "Told Daniel Coughlin he might have two days to get Maurice out of the village and if I knew of his being in the village for one year, I would turn him off."

The workday for Damon meant dealing with rowdiness, brawls, and drunk-

---

Overleaf: "Augustine Folsom has been here and taken views of the mill," Edward Damon wrote
in his diary on 16 September 1867. The clarity and depth perspective of the photo
during the early days of photography makes it probable that it was professionally taken.
(Courtesy of the Damon family)

en episodes. "Was sent for before I was up on account of Hartnet who was smashing things in a drunken spree." His supervision of the behavior of his employees extended beyond the confines of the workplace and incorporated a paternalistic sense of authority. "Hand came into office with a bottle of rum which I persuaded him to give to me," he wrote. "I called at his house just before dinner." Disapprovingly, he observed that two of his workers "Brown and Hawksworth last night stopped at the Junction till after eleven and sent no word to their wives."

After having been in the office most of the day, Damon on his return home was interrupted by a drunken dispute. "Just as I was coming up to the house there was a row in the store. I put Cassidy out and Smith took Ryan. They were drunk with Coburn. Gave John Puffer a pretty plain talk though he was hardly in a condition to appreciate it." Following a talk with a worker about to be discharged for his drinking, Damon decided to give him another chance "if he would go to Temperance Meeting this evening and make confession and sign pledge for one year." When the occasion demanded, Damon delivered the warning against drinking himself. "I have spent the morning talking to men about using liquor, while my watchman who has been away several days has had a spree and is off duty." Out of necessity Damon filled in as acting watchman for part of the night.

Turnover was high in the management of the boarding house adjacent to the mill on Water Street, run by women or couples who frequently stayed less than a year. Taking in boarders was a way for a woman to earn money when such opportunities were restricted. Anne Damon's unmarried sister Sarah Hagar ran a boarding house in Weston, which averaged five boarders. She complained about its demands. In her 1887 diary Sarah Hagar wrote: "Boarders are too much for me—I wish I need never have any more—then I could act myself and go my way and keep peace of mind." "I felt the burden of boarders awfully today—the anxiety about the table and not help enough." Perennially in search of "a girl" to assist her, Hagar often took the train to Boston to do the hiring and just as often was disappointed that the individual failed to show

---

The Damon Mill amidst rural surroundings.
Children play along the banks of the Assabet River. 1867.
(Courtesy of the Damon family)

A page from Edward Damon's 1881 memoranda book relate manufacturing data, weather, child labor and safety regulations.
(Courtesy of the Damon family)

up, performed poorly, or stayed for only a short period of time. Getting satisfactory domestic help was a problem her sister Anne shared as well. There was no workday that year on September 5 when Sarah Hagar recorded, "this was a new holiday called Labor Day."

Edward Damon was often needed to intervene in disturbances at the boarding house. "Mrs. Murray gave two men notice to leave the boarding house and I had them in the office." "Called to the boarding house to deal with a drunken spinner. I ordered him to leave." Another time Damon went "to see a girl who was accused of taking some money. Did not find money though think the girl took it."

"Am short of help as many have the measles," Damon remarked following an after-dinner walk to the tenement housing on High Street to check on his workers. During another evening walk through the village, he was forced to return to the mill, "having heard John Buckley was drunk and had insulted Gertie Javitt. I tried to get him home but as he would not go arrested him and took him down to lock up. Ralph went with me." And when "Levi Farwell in a drunken row struck Frank and said he would kill Mrs. Farwell if he could get hold of her, I swore out a warrant for his arrest. Had Levi Farwell before Judge Keyes who put him on probation."

His observations of worker productivity took a sardonic tone. "Mullins quit work after I told him we should expect more work and less resting on the shovel handle." "Spent most of the day in the office but have had several opportunities to rake down some of the men." "Killgore came down to see if he could be off for a few days and I asked him if he did not wish to be off longer at which he flew like a piece of glass."

While some operatives clearly felt that Damon kept too watchful an eye on them, frank talk did not mean dismissal. "Had a little blow with Page this morning as he thought I watched him too close." "Hunt quit because he would not work for a man who kept looking after him." "Chaplin's notice is out and he took occasion to tell me his opinion of me. Also that I overpaid a man $10 to show my fallibility." Further discussion resolved the impasse with an increase in pay.

Poor work meant a deduction of wages. "Michael Flynn broad loom weaver quit because he was discounted for weaving light," read the entry of 14 May 1880 with a follow-up three days later. "I had a talk with Michael Flynn who saw the matter of discount in a different light from what he had seen before.

We charged him 15 cents for what we had to pay $3.00." But Damon also accommodated his workers by giving them time off to attend local events. "The operatives wished to go to the Walden Pond Band Picnic this afternoon" and "have had a part of the mill stopped to let the boys go to the circus."

While no ledgers of Edward Damon's are known to survive, his diaries include references to wages paid. "Hired Michael O'Neil for four months at $20 plus board," he wrote in 1864. N.A. Wetherbee and his wife were hired in 1866 to run the boarding house at $20 per month. Twenty-nine letters of application were received in response to an 1869 advertisement for a night watchman and Nathaniel Stevens was hired at $12 per week. In 1870 the spinner A. Hawksworth was hired at $2.50 a day, but a year later he was fired. Damon wrote: "Turned Hawksworth the spinner off as he was the leader of six who came with complaints about the work." "Thomas Henry Ingham, age 15, will work in office for first year for 75 cents per day, second year for $1 per day . . . and Daniel Sheehan will work for a month for $1.75 per day and as I want him through the season," Damon noted in 1873.

Sometimes there was a trial period set when a worker began. In March 1875 he hired "Michael Burke to work for one year at $36 per month and house rent." "He to be on trial for one month and if each is satisfied to continue through the year." "Told Puffer I would pay him 10 cents an hour and would give him house rent for chores . . . Offered Butterworth 16 cents per hour on wool dresser . . . Alexander Brown was hired for $2.25 and let him have Twin Cottage #1 for $6 per month" [1877]. In 1881 Fletcher and Haynes were listed as receiving $2.50 a day for laying stone.

Damon's workers, including women, did approach him for pay increases. "Had a long talk with Lizzie Owens this morning about her pay," he wrote in 1881, but Damon set the tone under which discussion could take place. "Lovell came in quite an excited state. Wanted his pay increased. Told him when he was calm would talk with him" [1874]. In 1872 Damon related that he had a talk on labor reform with operatives Hinchcliffe and Hawksworth, the latter of whom proved troublesome by organizing worker opposition.

Once hired, mill operatives faced pay cuts. "Put up notices of reduction in wages," Damon noted matter of factly in his diaries. "Talked with overseers and plan to reduce wages. Decided on reduction of 10 percent till I can make sale of goods, find it meets their approval," Damon wrote in February 1862. The next day he held a meeting of all workers to explain the reason for the reduced pay and too optimistically stated, "believe all are satisfied." But instead there was "trouble in the wool room, spinner leaves and two girls asked for more pay." When a spinner left without giving advanced notice, Damon refused to pay him. Finding a qualified replacement did not always prove easy. "Harper went to Rock Bottom this morning to get a spinner and brought back a dog. He has been to Assabet this afternoon and has the promise of one tomorrow."

Skilled operatives in spinning and weaving united and at times walked off the job, though it was not unusual for them to "take back their notices" after a few days. "The spinners quit work this morning but all went back again, except one that I paid off" [November 1863]. When faced with such protest, Damon generally was resolute not to give in. "Was waited upon by the cotton spinners for more pay but did not grant it" [30 January 1864]. "Rose at 6 o'clock, was met on going to the factory by a large delegation each preferring charges against the others but I dismissed them all summarily" [21 July 1865].

Though no strikes are mentioned at Damon's mill, the ferment of worker opposition grew in the 1870s and Damon noted occasions when operatives refused his bid to work overtime. On 16 March 1874, he noted, "learn the Assabet Manufacturing Company employees are on a strike." Despite this strike among one thousand operators taking place so close-by, a week later Damon posted a notice for reduction of wages. On 30 January 1864 he recorded: "Was waited upon by the cotton spinners for more pay but did not grant it." Indeed two weeks later he reduced wages for spinners at the same time observing that "weavers have been out most of the day."

Once decided, the task of dismissal was carried out with firmness by Damon. "Spent nearly all the morning in one of the most disagreeable of duties and have discharged two families and two private individuals." "Told Wilbur that we should not want him after a fortnight. Told Mr. Stevens that we could get along without him after this month, and let Houghton go." Preceding the dismissal of the spinner A. Hawksworth in December 1875, Damon kept memoranda notes. "October 5—25 minutes late in the morning and did not beam off two beams of yarn for broad looms till 10:30 a.m. . . . October 6— eight minutes late . . . December 15—took ¾ hour for breakfast."

The sharp explosions of the nearby Powder Mills were heard at Damon's factory and the tragic consequences soon became known. "Powder mill blew up at

11:10 a.m. and Mr. Taylor was so terribly burned that he died before 5 p.m." At Damon's mill, workers similarly fell victim to the very machinery created to assist them, mangled, maimed, and absorbed by its power.

Unlike the absentee owner, Damon's presence on site made him aware of those who fell victim. "Frank Farwell had his little finger taken off in a gear this morning . . . Minerva Shattuck ran her finger through a gear . . . Hawksworth cut his wrist badly on the Empire loom . . . Maggie Fallon hurt one of her fingers . . . Frank Puffer got his hand caught in the dryer."

"Frank Fletcher met with a fearful accident at about three this afternoon. His right hand was severed from the arm and the arm broken so that it was amputated at the shoulder from being caught by a belt and carried around by the shaft. Anne was at the Fletchers till eight o'clock." Fletcher was later given seventy-five dollars by Damon, a significant donation at a time when there was no workmen's compensation or severance pay.

Mortality was high among young children, and Damon was sensitive to their untimely deaths. Families of the prominent and the poor felt the grief; they were the offspring of his workers as well as two of his own children. Damon was actively involved with the burial arrangements of the children including measuring and securing the coffin. "Jackman's little girl died this morning" [1865]. "Went over to Jackman's and took measurements for casket and went up to South Acton to order it. Jackman's twins were buried this afternoon."

"Another of Fitzsimmons children was buried today. . . ." "Mr. Robbins daughter died of scarlet fever. . . ." "Dr. [Edward] Emerson has a son. . . ." But three days later on 14 July 1875, "Dr. Emerson's little boy is dead." And of his longtime bookkeeper's loss he wrote, "Potter was here his little boy only lived six days."

When a child was born out of wedlock to a twenty-year-old mill operative from Ireland, Damon's 1862 diary included comment of how beautiful the daughter of Ellen Sullivan was. Anne Damon visited the mother to see the baby and ask if she was keeping the child. Soon after appeared one final reference, "Ellen Sullivan and child taken to Tewksbury," the location of one of three state almshouses.

I Built Up a Village

Throughout the summer of 1881 the nation awaited news of the fate of Pres. James Garfield, inaugurated on March 4 and shot on July 2 by disappointed office seeker Charles Guiteau. During August the news of the president was "very alarming," as his condition deteriorated. "For a fortnight hopes and fears have nearly balanced in regard to the President but tonight it seems as if nothing but a miracle can save him," Damon wrote on August 27. Work stopped for an hour at the mill on September 2 to hold "prayers for the President." Ten days later, Damon noted Sergeant John Mason attempted to shoot Guiteau in his cell. The vigil ended the following week on September 19, "Pres. Garfield dies at Long Branch at 10:35 this evening." Throughout Concord, he observed, "there is hardly a store that has not some evidences of mourning and many are very elaborate." Memorial services were held for the late president on September 26. "We all went to town this afternoon and attended."

The last surviving diary of Edward Damon from 1881 continued its blend of events—business and personal, national and local. In July, Anne Damon attended the season's opening of Bronson Alcott's School of Philosophy at the Orchard House, Edward was elected one of the directors of the Pemberton Mills in Lawrence and bemoaned a lack of worker productivity at his own mill. "Almy wrote me a pretty sharp letter on production. I never worked so hard for 6 months with such poor results. I never knew such a time with help . . ." "Turned Fred Rand off this morning," he wrote on September 12. Two days later, "Rand came back and after a good talk I let him go to work. I told Hawkins that if he did not do better I should have to get someone else. His mistakes are too frequent and unnecessary. Did not leave office till after 10:30

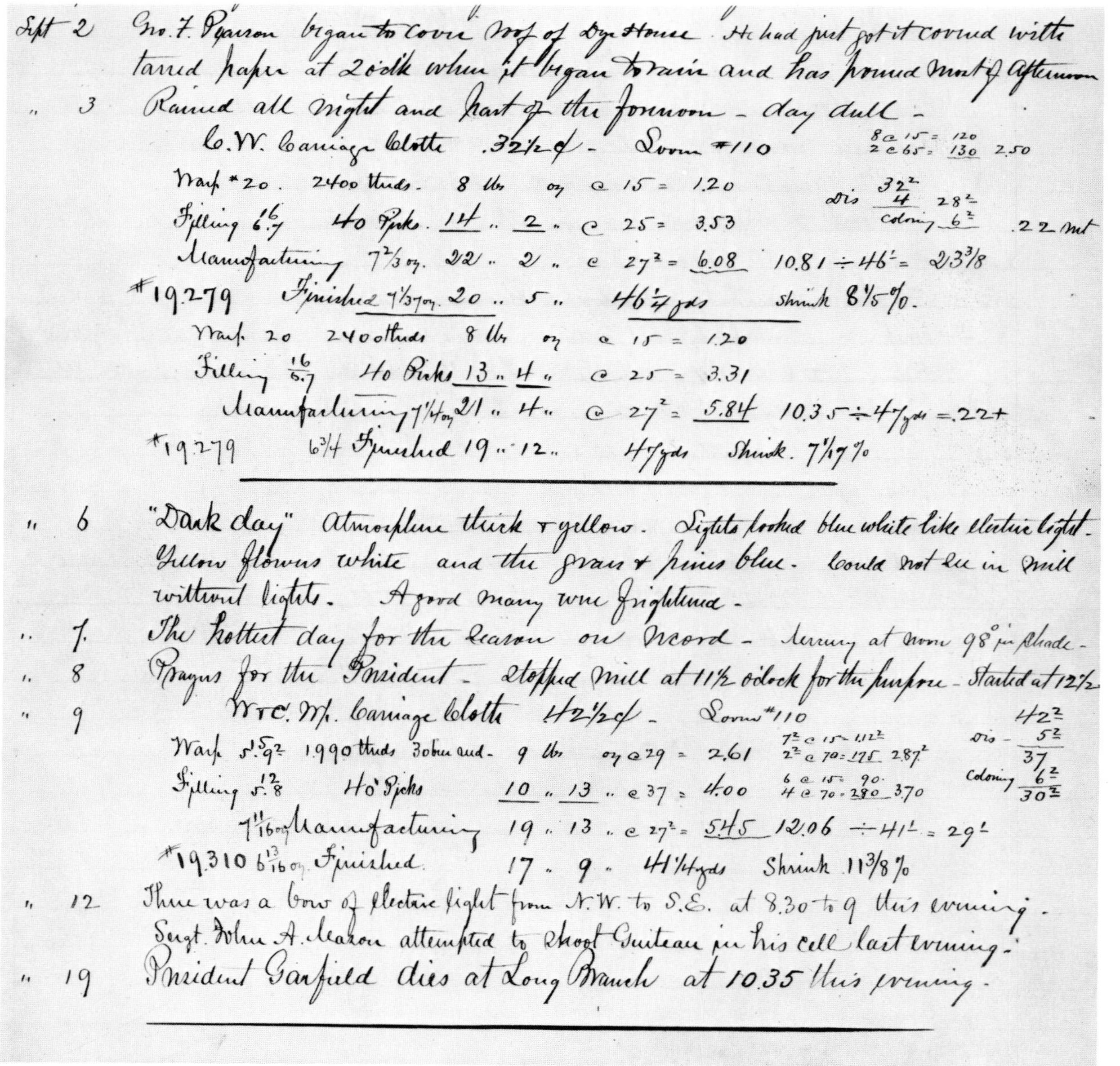

Sept 2 Geo. F. Pearson began to cover roof of Dye House. He had just got it covered with tarred paper at 2 o'clk when it began to rain and has poured most of afternoon

" 3 Rained all night and part of the forenoon — day dull —

C.W. Carriage Cloth .32½ c — Loom #110 8 @ 15 = 120 2 @ 65 = 130 2.50

Warp #20. 2400 thds — 8 lbs oz @ 15 = 1.20 Dis 32² 4 28²

Filling 16/6.7 40 Picks. 14 .. 2 .. @ 25 = 3.53 Coloring 6² .22 net

Manufacturing 7⅔ oz. 22 .. 2 .. @ 27² = 6.08 10.81 ÷ 46¼ = 23⅜

#19279 Finished 7⅓ oz. 20 .. 5 .. 46¼ yds Shrink 8⅘ %.

Warp 20 2400 thds 8 lbs oz @ 15 = 1.20

Filling 16/6.7 40 Picks 13 .. 4 .. @ 25 = 3.31

Manufacturing 7¼ oz 21 .. 4 .. @ 27² = 5.84 10.35 ÷ 47 yds = .22+

#19279 6¾ Finished 19 .. 12 .. 47 yds Shrink 7 1/17 %

" 6 "Dark day" Atmosphere thick & yellow. Lights looked blue white like electric light. Yellow flowers white and the grass & pines blue. Could not see in mill without lights. A good many were frightened.

" 7 The hottest day for the season on record — Mercury at noon 98° in shade —

" 8 Prayers for the President — Stopped mill at 11½ o'clock for the purpose — Started at 12½

" 9 W.C. M. Carriage Cloth 42½ c — Loom #110 42²

Warp 5 15/92 1990 thds 30 bu end — 9 lbs oz @ 29 = 2.61 7² @ 15 = 1.12² 2² @ 70 = 1.75 2.87² Dis 5² 37

Filling 5 12/8 40 Picks 10 .. 13 .. @ 37 = 4.00 6 @ 15 = 90 4 @ 70 = 280 370 Coloring 6² 30²

7 11/16 oz Manufacturing 19 .. 13 .. @ 27² = 5.45 12.06 ÷ 41¼ = 29¼

#19310 6 13/16 oz. Finished 17 .. 9 .. 41¼ yds Shrink 11⅜ %

" 12 There was a bow of electric light from N.W. to S.E. at 8.30 to 9 this evening. Sergt. John A. Mason attempted to shoot Guiteau in his cell last evening.

" 19 President Garfield dies at Long Branch at 10.35 this evening.

News of a mortally wounded president, and an attempt on the assassin's life, share space with weather developments and the making of cloth in this 1881 record of Edward Damon. [Courtesy of the Damon family]

p.m."[14 September]. "Crowley is off & sick & McNally is on a drunk. Went to see McNally this morning and then went to town and swore out warrant," he wrote on October 25. The following day, "took Hawkins and Pat McNally downtown this morning & McNally was put on probation for 60 days." His own efforts were exhaustive. "Worked on dryer till I was wet through so had to change my flannel" [28 October].

Drenched with the sweat of his labor, Damon's influence was evident in the workers that he employed and housed, the school enrollment, the company store with its post office, and the neighborhood fire fighting effort. By the close of the century, Edward Damon was able to say with veracity, "I built up a village."

The marvel of transmitting a voice by telephone was a new use of electricity and among the rapid technological advances of the era. "Some telephone poles were dropped along the road this afternoon," Damon noted on 19 November 1880. On December 24 a telephone was installed in his office which had its initiation three days later. "Telegraphed Almy and got reply from Junction by telephone, the first time we have used it." The next day he phoned his mother and was able to speak with her, a sister, and three of his childen who were visiting. "Mother also talked to me," he exclaimed.

Spurred by the building of the Fitchburg Railroad in 1844, with a stop near the Damon Mill, and the Framingham and Lowell in 1872, the town's industrial base grew. The intersection between the railroads formed "the Junction" stop at Commonwealth Avenue, and by 1900 West Concord accounted for three-quarters of the town's growth. Damon's mill was part of the mix of nineteenth-century industry that included the nation's first commercially produced pencils by William Munroe of Barrett's Mill Road during the War of 1812, the manufacture of lead pipe and sheet lead by David Loring in 1819, the successive use of the same Nashoba Brook site in 1857 by the wooden Pail Factory and the enlargement of the dam to form Warner's Pond by owner Ralph Warner, the industries of the state prison, Harvey Wheeler's Boston Harness Company which moved to the Junction in 1890, and George Conant's Bluine Manufacturing Company to whiten laundry, which opened in 1895 on the present Beharrell Street.

Though the Damon Mill for much of the nineteenth century was the town's largest employer, Damon eschewed the trappings of power that accompanied the position in contrast to Ralph Warner who also owned extensive property

Interior of Harvey Wheeler's Boston Harness Shop and a rare photo of its women employees. Circa 1895. (Courtesy of Jane and Richard Montague)

in West Concord. The Warner building on Commonwealth Avenue was used as a meeting place for social and religious groups and as the location of the Warnerville Post Office in 1877. Warner gave the land for the West Concord School built in 1886 and proposed that the street abutting the property be named after him. Instead, town meeting in 1894 chose to name it "Church Street" for the newly built West Concord Union Church. Resident petitioners succeeded on 1 July 1891 in naming the post office Concord Junction, the same as the railroad station, despite Warner's objection. The proprietor of the Pail Factory pressed further that the Junction area be called Warnerville. "Mr.

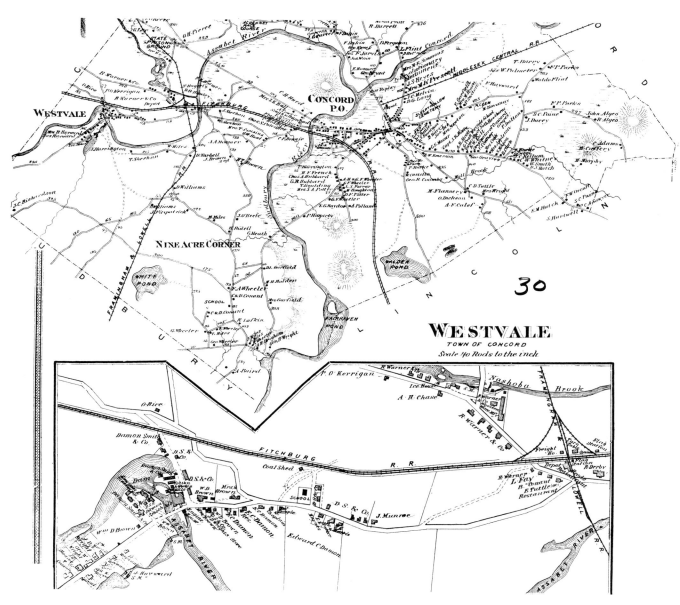

The textile mill and wooden pail factory dominated the town's industry
at the time of the centennial, and revealed the extensive property
holdings of owners Edward Damon and Ralph Warner.
(Courtesy of the Concord Free Public Library)

A lone figure walks past the mill on Main Street. Telephone poles,
the house built by Col. Roger Brown, the Westvale bridge, and the outline of housing
on the hill block, can be seen. January 1887. (Courtesy of the Damon family)

I BUILT UP A VILLAGE

Pierce Clark at prison came to see me about protesting against change of Concord Junction to Warnerville," Damon noted in his diary on 21 April 1880.

By contrast, when Edward Damon was approached to have the post office across from the mill called Damondale, he declined the honor. In his memoirs Henry Smith recalled: "The mill had become well known as 'Damondale Mill,' and it seemed to myself as well as many others that that should be the name; Mr. Damon felt that it would be rather presuming on his part to fasten his name to the village. . . . At his solicitation I invited several gentlemen to meet us at my house on the evening of 8 December 1870, at which time several names were suggested and duly considered, and before we separated the present name, Westvale, was decided upon." The first delivery of mail at the Westvale Post Office was on 31 January 1871. The arrival and transport of mail shipments was determined by the schedule of trains that stopped at the Conant Street crossing.

"Damon's pride," related Henry Smith, "was in the improvement, growth and prosperity of that part of town which had been his home from infancy." On the evening of 8 March 1881 at 7:30, a meeting was called for the purpose of forming a "Village Improvement Association." Seventeen members including Anne Damon came to the mill in the hall above the counting room, and Edward Damon was appropriately elected president. Ten dollars paid in one sum bought a life membership as did five dollars paid annually for two years. Otherwise the cost was fifty cents for anyone fifteen years and over and twenty-five cents annually if younger. According to the constitution drawn up, "its objects shall be, firstly—in summer, to improve the streets and grounds by planting and cultivating trees, cleaning and repairing sidewalks, and doing such other acts as shall tend to beautify and adorn said streets. Secondly—in winter, to plan and encourage means of mutual and social improvement." At the May 12 meeting membership had grown to twenty-seven and there were fifteen dollars in the treasury. Some of the names listed in attendance are recognizable from the census as workers at the mill, while others like Abiel Chase owned considerable property in the area. By the close of the century, membership had narrowed to the Damon family, and the association was disbanded following a special meeting held on 19 September 1896.

The membership book retained by Damon noted that the Association planted trees along Main Street, requested extra street lamps, made repairs to the Westvale schoolhouse, and graded the yard. Complaints were registered about horses injuring shade trees and compliance requested from offending drivers.

"Will you please caution your drivers against allowing their horses to injure the shade trees in our village," wrote the Westvale Village Improvement Association Secretary, W. A. Wright, to Tuttles, Jones and Wetherbee livery. "We have organized an association for the improvement of our streets and as some of our members recently saw one of your horses browsing a tree it was voted at our last meeting to call your attention to the subject." The same message was sent to the drivers of Mr. Edwin Gilman, with the added warning that "the statute makes the owner of the horse liable for the injury done."

For diversion, members chose teams for debate and voted for the winning side on such topics as "who was the greater man Washington or Franklin?" or "which is the most useful metal gold or iron?" Washington emerged the greater man and iron the more useful metal despite Damon's advocacy for gold.

Eclipse

On 6 December 1898 Edward Damon appeared before a meeting of his fellow trustees at the Middlesex Institution for Savings. He had served on the board since 8 June 1869, but this time he came as a supplicant, attempting to ward off foreclosure of the mill.

The handwritten draft of Damon's address to his fellow trustees was saved by his daughter Alice in an envelope she marked "very valuable." She noted that the "contents might be useful as an indicator of character and accomplishment as well as historical facts."

Pride and supplication alternate in this powerful record of his appearance. The purpose of his request was "that if possible I may be saved the mortification and expense of bankruptcy. I do not ask you to consider this other than on business principles. I wish to say here and now that I am not going to make this a personal matter . . . I have been on this board longer than most of you, I know how business has been done here . . .

"You will I feel all admit that the present condition in which I am placed towards this institution is not the result of any attempt on my part to defraud, or the result of speculation. A great shadow has come over the textile industry of our country. One political party says it is our tariff—the other says it is because we have allowed foreigners to get possession of our markets. Whatever the cause we are confronted with the condition.

"It will be forty-five years in five weeks since my father died and left me the oldest of seven children—seventeen and a half years old—I had been at home a year and a half working at various jobs in the mill and keeping my fathers books. For more than forty years I was at the head of the business in what is now known as the Village of Westvale. During that time I paid out nearly $2

"Concord Enterprise," 25 March 1892.

"Concord Enterprise," 14 May 1896.

"Concord Enterprise," 19 November 1896.

Advertisements of the Damon Mill that appeared regularly during the 1890's,
revealed the diverse selection and high style of the cloth made.

million in wages. I put nearly $400,000 into real estate and machinery. I built up a village. I paid my taxes promptly and without complaint. One year I paid one dollar out of every eleven dollars raised. I believe it to be true that I have paid more money into the treasury of the Town than any other man.

"I have lived honestly, modestly and when I had the means gave liberally. I paid as good wages as any manufacturer and had the respect and confidence of my employees and the love of a large number. Nothing is more trying to me than to be unable to pay my debts but I stand before you in this condition. I simply ask that you shall consider this subject fully and then act in the way which will enable you to get the most out of my property. If you decide it is by bankruptcy I can endure the publicity and disgrace. If I can give you as much as you can realize by that course and save the expense: I trust you will take such action as will enable me to do so." But the foreclosure proceedings which had begun earlier in the year had reached their final stages.

In July 1889 the mill property had been mortgaged to the Middlesex Institution for Savings for $50,000 for five years when the Damon Manufacturing Company was formed as a family corporation with Ralph Damon as president and Edward as the treasurer, a position where the source of power rested. The mill was never able to recover from the economic depression of 1893. In addition the expansion of the mill to make dress goods was an expensive change, while knitted underwear had reduced the demand for white flannels.

In 1894 when he was elected president of the Concord National Bank, Edward Damon gave his interest in the mill property to his son Ralph. The following spring his health weakened when he suffered "several severe hemorrhages" according to Smith who described his cousin at this time as "a suffering invalid, unable to give personal attention to the details of manufacturing."

The finances of the mill continued to deteriorate and with the mortgage in arrears the Middlesex Institution for Savings, after several postponements, foreclosed on 1 March 1898 though bank records show continued efforts

---

Overleaf: The Assabet River and the tracks of the Fitchburg Railroad behind the Damon Mill.
Steam-powered engines no longer limited mill owners to the river's geography.
Transportation of goods by railroads and cheaper labor to the South,
ended New England dominance of the textile mills. Late nineteenth century.
(Courtesy of the Concord Free Public Library)

through the year to avert its permanence. The bank's ledgers show that foreclosure was first threatened in 1896 but a loan that September was made to the property for $6,500 at 5 percent interest using as collateral the Damon property of "the William Brown House, the hill block, the company store, the French Roof cottage and lots of land with the same provided that he will apply the same upon the mortgage now held by this institution." The following December the investment committee of the bank was authorized to pay the overdue taxes on the property. The final report of the committee of investment on 20 September 1899 reported that a settlement in full had been made with Edward Damon by his payment of $2,275 while the amount of $3,424 represented the loss on the mortgage and was charged to the Guaranteer Fund.

Henry Smith recalled the money and effort that Edward Damon put into the mill as an investment for his children's future. "I don't intend to have my children go through what I have. I am doing the job in such a manner that they will not have to do it over again after I am gone."

But Damon's mill fell victim to the general decline of the textile industry in New England and Smith painfully observed the end. "To see it all go, and the industry into which he put his very life in building up entirely wiped out, was more than most men could have endured."

When foreclosure came, the property was advertised and, according to Smith, sold on 7 April 1898 for $40,100 at public auction to the legal representative of the bank, the sole bidder. The following year the officers of the bank decided to sell the machinery to a second-hand dealer "for a sum that in some years was no larger than repair costs to the plant," related Smith. The mill and water power were sold to the Concord Rubber Company, makers of drug supplies, mackintoshes, and rubber footwear for less than Calvin Damon paid for it over sixty-five years before. Smith viewed the transaction as "unwise disposal of such a valuable manufacturing property over Damon's earnest protest, at a time when all business was in a very unsettled condition. . . ."

The Concord Junction Investment Company, controlled by John Studley and George Russell, purchased the outside real estate that included twenty tenements. The rubber company remained for about five years when the Strathmore Worsted Mills, makers of fine worsteds and serges and part of the American Woolen Company, occupied the mill until 1923.

By the close of the century, the manufacturing of clothing was transformed from a home-based industry to a mature factory system. Steam-powered engines no longer made the mill owner dependent on a specific river location; railroads added to the mobility of transporting goods, and owners followed cheaper labor costs to the South.

In life Edward Damon had shared the labor of the factory; in death he succumbed to "tuberculosis pulmonalis," an affliction common to its workers. A lifelong friendship existed between Edward Damon and Henry Smith's sister Mary Bliss. In their youth they vowed to exchange letters on January 12, the anniversary of Calvin Damon's death, describing the year that had past, and throughout their life they kept this promise. Damon struggled without success to dictate one last letter to her before he died at his Stow Street home on 13 January 1901. The following day her letter arrived. Unexpectedly, one month later Mary Bliss died.

Following his death, a committee of the Concord Antiquarian Society, which he helped found in 1886, wrote in tribute: "The Concord Antiquarian Society desires to place upon its records some expression of the loss it has sustained in common with the rest of this community in the death of Edward Carver Damon. Assuming while yet in his teens a responsible and arduous position in business, from which many a man of more years and experience and less of courage and fixity of purpose might well have shrunk, his whole life fully justified the confidence he then felt in himself and that his neighbors and friends came to repose in him. In every relation of life, in his family, in his church, in his social duties, in the countless positions of trust and of labor to which his fellow citizens were continually calling him, his good sense, his uprightness, and his readiness to do all and more than was required of him, constantly approved themselves. Nothing that was good in the town of Concord but found in him a forwarder and a friend. No duty was beneath him, no right thing was unworthy of his notice and of his aid. In this society, of which he was one of the originators, and a life member, the worthy qualities of his character were as evident as in everything else, and until the infirmities of a long and painful illness made activity almost impossible and work a burden, he was always ready to do all that he could to further its objects and aid in its success. We regret our own loss, and tender our sympathies to his wife and children in theirs."

Edward Damon was buried at Sleepy Hollow Cemetery, in the family plot located alongside that of his friend Ralph Waldo Emerson. At the time of his death, his eight surviving children were Ralph Hagar, an insurance agent born 3 October 1861; Mary Bliss, a physician in Minneapolis, Minnesota, born 2 August 1863; Harriet Lincoln Taylor, a resident of South Orange, New Jersey, born 12 March 1865; Alice Harper, a principal at the Mystic Oral School for the Deaf in Mystic, Connecticut, born 11 October 1867; William Cotton, a mill superintendent in Franklin, New Hampshire, born 30 August 1870; Robert Gibbs, an assistant mill superintendent in North Andover, Massachusetts, born 15 August 1879; John Churchill, a student at the Massachusetts Institute of Technology, born 30 March 1882; and Theron Johnson, a student at Harvard College, born 25 February 1883. The two children who had died in infancy were Rebekah Cotton, born 15 June 1872, died 26 April 1875, and Helen Farnham, born 18 September 1884, died 9 February 1885.

Of all Edward Damon's children, Ralph received the most attention in his father's diaries, which chronicled his development from infancy to manhood. It was a course that traversed boyhood mischief and a seemingly stubborn bent to disobey, to the independence of an adult male and his anticipated succession as head of the family business.

Perhaps Ralph lacked his father's business acumen and disciplined work habits to withstand the adverse economic conditions of the last decade of the century. Local newspaper advertisements show his flair for salesmanship and effort at opening a short-lived retail store on Commonwealth Avenue to sell the mill's remnant goods. Ralph married in 1884, and he and his wife Mary lived in the house built for them on land donated by his parents next to their own home. The house continues to be lived in by his descendants. Following his father's death, Ralph moved to New York City where he worked as an insurance agent.

The century had closed on the mill run by three generations of Damons. It was here, at the site of one of the earliest cotton mills in the nation, that the Industrial Revolution came to Concord and domet cloth became an American staple. And it was during the cultural flowering of New England and Concord's golden literary period that a manufacturer of cloth walked in the company of philosopher kings.

Bibliography

DAMON FAMILY COLLECTION

Damon, Anne Hagar. Letters, 1877, 1878. Private collection.

Damon, Anne Hagar family. Diary, 1860, belonging to unidentified family member. Private collection.

Damon, Calvin Carver. Account books, 1834-1837. Private collection.

Damon, Edward Carver. Diaries, 1862-1881; miscellaneous letters, business documents, and record books, 1877–1898. Private collection.

Hagar, Sarah. Diary, 1887. Private collection.

Smith, Henry Francis. "Edward Carver Damon." In *Memoirs of Members of the Social Circle* in Concord. 4th ser. Cambridge, Mass.: Riverside Press, 1909.

————. Autobiographical manuscript circa 1900 and miscellaneous letters, 1850–1877. Private collection.

Smith, Henry Francis Jr. "Henry Francis Smith." In *Memoirs of Members of the Social Circle in Concord.* 5th ser. Cambridge, Mass.: University Press, 1940.

GENERAL REFERENCE

Bagnall, Willam M. "Contributions to American Economic History," 1908. Museum of American Textile History, North Andover, Mass.

The Blue Book Textile Directory of the U.S. and Canada. [New York]: Davison Publishing. 1889–1899.

Bolles, Albert. *Industrial History of the United States.* Norwich,Conn.: Henry Bill Publishing, 1879.

Brown, Percy. "Charles Edward Brown." In *Memoirs of Members of the Social Circle in Concord.* 5th ser. Cambridge, Mass.: University Press, 1940.

Buell, Laurence. *Literary Transcendentalism: Style and Vision in the American Renaissance.* Ithaca, N.Y.: Cornell University Press, l973.

Cole, Arthur Harrison. *The American Wool Manufacture.* Cambridge, Mass.: Harvard University Press, 1926.

Massachusetts, Commonwealth of. "Statistics of Certain Branches of Industry, as they existed in the Town of Concord 1865." Concord Free Public Library, Concord, Mass., 1865.

Concord, Mass. Concord Births, Marriages, and Deaths, 1635–1850. Town, 1891.

Concord Directories. Boston: Thomas Todd Printer. 1892–1905.

Concord, Mass. "Concord Enterprise," 1880–1900.

Concord, Mass. *Reports of the Selectmen and School Committee.* Boston: Thomas Todd, Benjamin Tolman Printers. 1860–1900.

Concord, Mass. "Soldiers and Sailors of Concord Massachusetts 1861–1865," Concord Free Public Library. Concord, Mass.

Dee, Joseph & Son Funeral Home. Records. Concord, Mass.

Digital Equipment Corporation. "Digital's Mill, 1847–1977". Maynard, Mass.: Digital Equipment Corp., 1977.

Dublin, Thomas. *Women at Work: The Transformation of Work and Community in Lowell, Massachusetts, 1826–1860.* New York: Columbia University Press, 1979.

Dunwell, Steve. *The Run of the Mill.* Boston: David R. Godine, 1978.

Dwyer, Carol. "Community Spirit Evidenced in the Landscape: Concord and West Concord Centers in the Last Quarter of the Nineteenth and Twentieth Centuries." Concord, Mass., 1982.

Eno, Arthur, ed. *Cotton Was King: A History of Lowell, Massachusetts.* New Hampshire Publishing with the Lowell Historical Society, 1976.

Hammond, Charles. "Factory Village, Concord, Mass., 1654–1862." Ms., Concord Free Public Library, Concord, Mass., 1974.

Hurd, Hamilton D. *History of Middlesex County.* Philadelphia: J. W. Lewis, 1890.

Little, David. *America's First Centennial Celebration.* Boston: Houghton Mifflin, 1974.

Middlesex Institution for Savings. Trustee Books, 1889–1900. Concord, Mass.

Moss, Marcia, ed. *A Catalog of Thoreau's Surveys in the Concord Free Public Library.* Genesco, N.Y.: Thoreau Society, 1976.

"Report of the Committee Appointed by the Town to Procure a List of Names of Those Who Served in the Civil and Spanish-American Wars." Concord, Mass., 1908.

Richardson, Laurence E. "Concord Chronicles, 1865–1899." Ms., Concord Free Public Library, Concord, Mass., 1967.

———. "Westvale, Warnerville, and Prison Village." Ms., Concord Free Public Library, Concord, Mass., 1964.

———. *Concord River.* Barre, Mass.: Barre Publishers, 1964.

Thoreau, Henry D. *The Writings of Henry David Thoreau.* Edited by Bradford Torrey. Vols. 12, 18. Boston:Houghton Mifflin, 1906.

———. "Field Notes of Surveys Made Since November 1849." Concord Free Public Library, Concord, Mass.

Turley, Janice. "Westvale: Concord's Earliest Industrial Area." Ms., Concord Public Library, Concord, Mass., 1980.

United States. National Archives and Records Service. Population Schedules of the census of the United States 1860, 1870, 1880, Massachusetts Middlesex County/ National Archives and Records.

Wallace, Anthony. *Rockdale.* New York: Alfred Knopf, 1978.

Ware, Caroline F. *The Early New England Cotton Manufacture: A Study in Industrial Beginnings.* Reprint. New York: Johnson Reprint Company, 1966.

Wheeler, Ruth. "1775 House." Ms., Concord Free Public Library, Concord, Mass., n.d.

Index